CUB SCOUTS

YOUTH
PROTECTION

BEGINS WITH YOUTH PROTECTION

How to Protect Your
Children From Child Abuse:
A Parent's Guide

BOY SCOUTS OF AMERICA

DEAR PARENT

Welcome to SCOUTING! We are so pleased that you have decided to join our movement, and we look forward to working together with your family to raise leaders of character who will shape our future in a positive way.

Through Scouting, youth can develop strong connections and make important contributions to their families, their community, and society at large. We would like to congratulate you for choosing a program with the key ingredients for helping youth grow into competent, caring, and confident adults. Research about highly effective programs has shown that these ingredients are:

- Positive and sustained adult-youth relationships
- Youth activities that build life skills
- Youth participation in and leadership of valued community activities

The Scouting program significantly enhances opportunities for personal development, including higher grades, school engagement, self-esteem, and resilience. The program provides a safe environment where relationships are built with caring and competent adults, where youth are encouraged to take leadership of their development, and where useful life skills are acquired.

The programs of the BSA focus on developing leaders of character. We do this by presenting and reinforcing the values found in the Scout Oath and Scout Law. It is enormously important for our members to have a moral compass and a strong work ethic to go along with it. For more information on the benefits of Scouting, go to www.scouting.org/programs/.

To realize the potential of Scouting, it is critical that we take all possible steps to create and maintain a safe environment for all who participate. That involves understanding personal boundaries and knowing what appropriate behaviors are in Scouting. Research indicates one of the best deterrents against child abuse is an open and continuous conversation between parents and their children. The following information is offered to help your family establish and maintain a safe environment where you can prevent your child or another child from being abused. This information can also empower you to stop abuse as soon as possible and seek the necessary help. The Committee for Children recommends having the Hot Chocolate Talk to begin the conversation. (See "National Resources.")

Child abuse is something we would rather not talk about, or even think about, but we must. Many of us find it challenging and difficult to begin this conversation with our children, and the risk is that we might never get around to it. There are numerous factors that can lead to abuse. Together, you and your program leader must work together to ensure all Youth Protection and Health and Safety policies are understood and followed. For additional information, see "Additional BSA Resources" on page 26. **Your child is that important**. In fact, all of our children are that important. **Youth Protection Begins With YOU**.

The information you will read is not meant to scare you. It is meant to raise your awareness about many forms of abuse and how to recognize it and report it. It is part of the BSA's commitment to creating safe environments for all youth. The Centers for Disease Control, the Vision for Violence Prevention, and youth-serving medical facilities committed to preventing child maltreatment refer to child abuse as a public health epidemic. The BSA and other youth-serving organizations are committed to investing resources and engaging their top experts to end all forms of child abuse and maltreatment.

Using This Booklet

This booklet can't address all threats to personal safety for our children in and out of Scouting, but it will inform and empower you to better **recognize**, **respond** to, and **report** most forms of abuse and begin the conversation. The first section contains information for parents about child abuse and some tips for talking with your child about child abuse. In the second section, we put that knowledge to work with exercises for you to share with your child. Research shows that children whose parents talk to them about preventing abuse are better able to protect themselves and are more likely to tell if they are experiencing abuse or have been abused.

This conversation is the start of a dialogue between you and your child about personal safety awareness. As your child grows, look for opportunities to strengthen open communication and give them the reassurance that no matter how frightening something may be, you and other trusted adults are there to help.

WHAT EVERY PARENT SHOULD KNOW

Before we can understand what to do about abuse, we must understand what we mean by *abuse*. Children can experience abuse in many ways: neglect, physical abuse, sexual abuse, or emotional abuse. Often a child who is abused in one way is abused in multiple ways. When we protect a child from one form of abuse, such as neglect, we are often protecting the child from additional forms of abuse.

Abuse often occurs in the home by parents, stepparents, siblings, and other youth and/or caretakers. It also occurs in schools, churches, and youth-serving organizations. Regardless of what you have heard, there is no known profile of an abuser or child molester. However, there are behaviors that children exhibit that may be an indicator that the child is being abused. Abuse can occur despite our screening process, which includes criminal background checks, reference checks, and checks against the Volunteer Screening Database. For more information on the BSA's screening protocol, see the *Guide to Safe Scouting*, found at www.scouting.org.

The overall safety of your child is important to us. If you have any concerns about the safety of your child or the actions of leaders or parents, contact your local council Scout executive immediately.

In an emergency, when you are unable to reach the Scout executive, the BSA provides a 24-hour helpline: 1-844-SCOUTS1 (1-844-726-8871).

The Scouts First Helpline is a resource for incidents involving child abuse or serious risk of harm to children only. It is not for general information or questions.

For questions about training, policy interpretation, program, etc., please contact your Scout executive or Member Care at 972-580-2489.

Sexual Abuse

When an adult or older youth uses his or her authority to involve a child in any type of sexual activity, it is child sexual abuse. Sexual abuse is unwanted sexual activity, with persons using force, making threats, or taking advantage of victims not able to give consent. Another type of sexual abuse occurs when an adult or youth crosses clear boundaries in communications, or exposes the youth to alcohol, drugs, or pornography. Children can be at risk of sexual abuse anywhere there is access or opportunity, such as at home; at a neighbor's house; at school, field trips, and public events; and even in Scouting.

A common misconception about sexual abuse is that children are most likely to be abused by strangers. In fact, the abuser is usually someone the child knows and trusts, and most likely is known to you, the parent. These adults or youth are most often male, but females also can be offenders.

Sexual Abuse by Adults

Adults who abuse children may manipulate, bribe, coerce, threaten, or force a child into feeling like a partner in the sexual activity. They most often use a multistep "grooming" process that focuses on the child's needs and possibly on the child's parents as well. Adults who may sexually harm your child might offer free babysitting services or overnight trips, for example, or make friends with you to gain enough trust to be alone with the child.

Once the potential abuser has identified the target child, characteristically, the grooming process moves to what looks like harmless touching—such as hugging and massages—or exposure, and looking for chances to be alone with the child. The person usually seeks a child who craves affection or attention and makes that child feel special by spending a lot of time with them and giving gifts and money. All children are vulnerable to sexual abuse because of their innocence, naivete, and total trust in and dependence upon adults.

> A red flag is a leader who violates the BSA's Youth Protection policy of no one-on-one contact in Scouting and seeks one-on-one contact with youth, especially outside of the Scouting program and utilizing digital and social media for such contact.

When the individual senses that the child has become comfortable with physical contact and has an emotional bond, the physical contact becomes more intense. The individual may prey on the child's natural curiosity about sexuality and may say that they are helping or teaching them sex education. The individual may suggest playing inappropriate games. The grooming may involve violating rules, drinking alcohol, smoking cigarettes—all to create a "special relationship."

Most children don't know they are being groomed until it is too late.

Many abusers are clever enough to trick the victim into believing that they are equally to blame or will not be believed if they tell. Other abusers will manipulate the emotional bond and threaten to withhold love and attention if the child tells anyone. Many children feel trapped, overwhelmed, or ashamed and are afraid to tell.

Some children find it difficult to immediately report or disclose the abuse because of fear or love of the individual abusing them.

Sexual Abuse by Other Youth

It is also possible for a child of similar age or older to abuse another through force, position of authority, or manipulation. About a third of sexual abuse occurs at the hands of other children, including siblings, relatives, older youth, and youth in positions of authority and supervision who manipulate through bullying behavior using their size or authority. Overnight activities pose a greater risk of abuse including sleepovers, campouts, etc. Any peer activity, such as a club initiation or hazing, in which sexual activity is included, is a form of sexual abuse and should be addressed and reported immediately.

Adults who learn or discover that youth-on-youth abuse has occurred or who have concerns about youth exhibiting questionable, problematic, or illegal sexual behaviors must take immediate steps to stop it and report. Refer to www.ncsby.org as a resource·for additional information.

Responding/Reporting

If you suspect a child has experienced sexual abuse or has sexually abused other children inside or outside of Scouting, call 911 immediately and make a report *as required by your state and child protective services, or CPS.* Additional reporting may be required by your state.

Additionally, contact your local council Scout executive. If the Scout executive is unavailable, contact the Scouts First Helpline at 1-844-SCOUTS1 (1-844-726-8871).

Physical Abuse

Physical abuse is the deliberate injury of a child by a person responsible for the child's care.

Physical abuse injuries can include bruises, broken bones, burns, and scrapes. Children experience minor injuries as a normal part of childhood, usually in places such as the shins, knees, and elbows. When injuries do not seem to be the typical "bumps and bruises" of childhood or do not match the explanation given, it is possible that the child is being or has been abused.

Blows to the stomach may result in abdominal bruises, even if you can't see a mark. When a child complains of pain or says that they have been punched in the stomach, this should be taken seriously, because there may be internal injury.

The following signs are commonly associated with abuse but are not absolutes:

- Explanations of an injury, provided to you by a child or parent, that don't make sense
- Injuries on a child who has been absent from school or youth activities
- Complaints of soreness when moving
- Fear of going home with or to parents

Neglect

Neglect often involves depriving a child of food, clothing, shelter, medical care, or other necessities of life. Neglect can also involve exposing a child to harmful substances or materials, such as drugs, alcohol, or pornography, or to harmful practices such as violent behavior.

A number of clues suggest that a child might be neglected. The child who frequently comes to meetings with body odor, the child who is frequently unkempt, the child who is living in a dangerous environment, and the child with an obvious medical need that goes unattended all are showing signs that they could be neglected. So is the child who is always hungry or who hoards or steals food, the child who is seldom dressed appropriately for the weather, and the child who regularly talks of seeing a parent drunk or bruised from being hit.

Any time a child shows a need or condition that a reasonable parent would attend to—especially when failure to provide for the need harms the child's physical or emotional well-being— the child is likely being neglected.

Emotional Abuse

A child suffers from emotional abuse when continually ridiculed, blamed, humiliated, or compared unfavorably with others.

Emotional abuse damages the child's self-esteem. Studies find that emotional abuse is just as harmful as, if not more harmful than, other forms of abuse. It can lead to developmental problems, speech delays, depression, anxiety, and conditions such as low empathy and difficulty with friends.

Emotional abuse can occur when a parent completely ignores, rejects, or regularly threatens to beat a child, or when a child struggles to meet a parent's unreasonable expectations in academics, athletics, or other areas. Emotional abuse can also result if an adult or older youth provides a child with alcohol, drugs, pornography, or other harmful substances or materials.

Spiritual Abuse

An often-overlooked form of child maltreatment is spiritual abuse—the incorporation of religion into the abuse of a child. Some studies suggest that adults who abuse children are particularly attracted to faith communities because they find clergy and other faith leaders to be very trusting. If your child is active in a faith community, make sure to ask about what youth protection policies they have in place.

Youth With Developmental Disabilities/Special Needs

Children with disabilities or behavioral problems are at greater risk of abuse than other children. Adults who abuse children believe that youth with disabilities will be least likely to report the abuse. Accordingly, while it is important to teach all children to recognize would-be abusers and to tell a trusted adult about abuse, this message is particularly important for children with disabilities.

Special Considerations

It is vital that parents be forthcoming with unit leaders about any concerns or expectations you have about your child, as well as medication that may influence behavior.

Signs Your Child Might Have Been Abused

The clearest sign of abuse is that your child tells you that someone hurt or scared them or made them feel uncomfortable or you uncover evidence of abuse. Unfortunately, many children never speak of abuse, so it is important for you to maintain communications where your child can openly discuss matters of personal safety. Remember, reassuring them that they can tell you anything needs to be a continuous message you deliver.

If your child has been abused by a parent, relative, sibling, Scout, Scout leader, or someone else close to you, it may be particularly difficult for the child to disclose the abuse to you and also difficult for you to accept. Studies show that children rarely lie about sexual abuse or other maltreatment. So if your child tells you that they have been abused, or if your child is especially uncomfortable with a particular person or situation, always take the behavior as your sign to act. Remember, children communicate with us through their words, actions, and feelings. Communication about abuse is often subtle and indirect. A child may not come right out and say something; instead they may say, "I have a friend who ...," to see how an adult will react. The child who receives a helpful, thoughtful, and sympathetic response is more likely to reveal that they are not actually talking about their friend and tell you about abuse experiences. Listen carefully.

Each child's response to abuse is unique. Signs of stress frequently accompany abuse, but stress can have many causes. Other possible indicators of abuse include

- Sudden withdrawal from activities the child previously enjoyed
- Reluctance to be around or, especially, alone with a particular individual, adult or youth
- Changes in behavior or in school performance, including lower grades
- Inability to focus or learning problems with no known cause
- Hypervigilance (excessive watchfulness as if anticipating something bad happening)
- Overly compliant behavior or an excessive desire to please

In addition, a child currently being sexually abused may

- Have difficulty sitting or walking
- Complain of pain or itching in the genital or anal areas
- Use sexually explicit language or act out sexual behavior inappropriate for their age

For more information, take the BSA's Youth Protection Training at https://my.scouting.org.

Responding/Reporting

It is OK to ask a child about suspicious injuries or behaviors. In fact, you should. If the child tells of abuse or gives an answer that doesn't make sense and you feel the child is in danger, you should immediately contact the local law enforcement agency or state department of children and family services. You also need to contact your local council Scout executive. If your local council Scout executive is not available, contact the Scouts First Helpline at 1-844-SCOUTS1 (1-844-726-8871).

Scouts First Helpline

As part of its "Scouts First" approach to the protection and safety of youth, the BSA has established a dedicated 24-hour helpline to receive reports of known or suspected abuse or behavior that puts a youth at immediate risk.

In an emergency, when you are unable to reach the Scout executive, the BSA provides a 24-hour helpline: 1-844-SCOUTS1 (1-844-726-8871).

The Scouts First Helpline is a resource for incidents involving child abuse or serious risk of harm to children only. It is **not** for general information or questions.

For questions about training, policy interpretation, program, etc., please contact your Scout executive or Member Care at 972-580-2489.

1-844-SCOUTS1 (1-844-726-8871)

When to use it:

- Anytime you believe a youth has been harmed or their safety and well-being is at risk, and you cannot immediately reach your local council Scout executive or local council.

- If a Scout is bullied because of race, color, national origin, religion, sexual orientation, or disability, and local efforts are unable to resolve the problem.

If someone is at immediate risk of harm, always call 911.

For more information about reporting requirements, call 911 or see the Child Welfare Information Gateway website at www.childwelfare.gov for your state hotline number.

Bullying/Cyberbullying

Bullying is any intentional, aggressive behavior, often involving an imbalance of power or strength, that usually is repeated over a period of time. Bullying can take many forms, including hitting or punching, teasing or name calling, intimidating use of gestures or social exclusion, or sending insulting messages by phone or computer (cyberbullying). If your child is being targeted, do not blame your child or tell them to ignore the behavior or engage in physical retaliation. Instead, listen carefully and report the bullying behavior to the people responsible for the program where bullying is occurring. For more information, please see the BSA's Bullying Awareness webpage at www.scouting.org/training/youth-protection/bullying or www.stopbullying.gov.

Victims of bullying behavior are more likely to be depressed, have low self-esteem, be absent from school or other activities, feel sick, or think about death by suicide.

Any information indicating a youth has mentioned or talked about suicide must be taken seriously and reported to the Scout executive so appropriate actions may be taken. If unable to reach the Scout executive, contact the Scouts First Helpline at 1-844-SCOUTS1 (1-844-726-8871).

Internet/Social Media Safety

Today's youth are spending more time than ever using digital media for education, research, socializing, and fun. Unfortunately, abusers know this too. Parents play an important role in keeping children safe from those who use the internet and social media to access and harm children. Parents can limit the danger by setting basic guidelines such as when children go online, what sites they can visit, and having regular check-ins to see and discuss the choices that are being made with technology. To help families and volunteers keep youth safe while online, the BSA introduced the Cyber Chip.

In developing this tool, the BSA teamed up with content expert NetSmartz®, part of the National Center for Missing and Exploited Children® and training expert for many law enforcement agencies. Earning the Cyber Chip is a requirement for all Cub Scout ranks except Bobcat. For more information, please see the BSA's Cyber Chip webpage at www.scouting.org/training/youth-protection/cyber-chip and NCMEC's Netsmartz website at www.netsmartz.org. The NCMEC's CyberTipline number is 800-843-5678.

The BSA's Barriers to Abuse

Our goal in the BSA is to create and maintain a safe environment so that all can benefit from the program. The greatest positive step that we can take together is to put us all in a position to succeed by having rules that we all agree to follow. You should expect your child's Cub Scout pack to follow the Youth Protection policies put in place by the BSA to provide additional safety for your child and all who are involved in Scouting. These policies are helpful for anyone who works with or spends time with children who are not theirs, and not just in Scouting. They are practices used by teachers, doctors, camp counselors, coaches, and other adults who professionally work with children. Youth Protection policies and Health and Safety procedures continue to be updated regularly. For the most up-to-date information and changes or additions to policies and procedures, go to www.scouting.org/health-and-safety/gss.

You should discuss these policies with your child so that you, your child, and leaders have a shared understanding of what is expected in Scouting.

Leader Registration Requirements

The chartered organization representative, or in their absence the executive officer of the chartered organization, must approve the registration of the unit's adult leaders.

Registration includes:

- Completion of application including criminal background check and mandatory Youth Protection training

- Volunteer Screening Database check

Youth Protection training is required for leaders when renewing their registration or at unit charter renewal.

Adult program participants must register as adults and follow Youth Protection policies. Up-to-date Youth Protection and Health and Safety information is available at www.scouting.org/health-and-safety/gss.

Adult Supervision

Two registered adult leaders 21 years of age or over are required at all Scouting activities, including meetings. There must be a registered female adult leader 21 years of age or over in every unit serving females. A registered female adult leader 21 years of age or over must be present for any activity involving female youth. Notwithstanding the minimum leader requirements, age- and program-appropriate supervision must always be provided.

All adults accompanying a Scouting unit who are present at the activity for 72 total hours or more must be registered as leaders. The 72 hours need not be consecutive.

One-on-one contact between adult leaders and youth members is prohibited both inside and outside of Scouting.

- In situations requiring a personal conference, the meeting is to be conducted with the knowledge and in view of other adults and/or youth.
- Private online communications (texting, phone calls, chat, IM, etc.) must include another registered leader or parent.
- Communication by way of social media (Facebook, Snapchat, etc.) must include another registered leader or parent.

Discipline must be constructive.

- Discipline must reflect Scouting's values.
- Corporal punishment is never permitted.
- Disciplinary activities involving isolation, humiliation, or ridicule are also prohibited.

Responsibility

Leaders must ensure that all participating in Scouting activities abide by the Scout Oath and Scout Law.

Adult leaders and youth members share the responsibility for the safety of all participants in the program, including adherence to Youth Protection and Health and Safety policies.

- Adult leaders are responsible for monitoring behavior and intervening when necessary.

- Physical violence, sexual activity, emotional abuse, spiritual abuse, unauthorized weapons, hazing, discrimination, harassment, initiation rites, bullying, cyberbullying, theft, verbal insults, drugs, alcohol, and pornography have no place in the Scouting program and may result in revocation of registration.

All leaders are required to adhere to the Scouter Code of Conduct located in the *Guide to Safe Scouting*: www.scouting.org/health-and-safety/gss.

Accommodations

Separate accommodations for adult males and females and youth males and females are required.

Tenting

- Separate tenting arrangements must be provided for male and female adults as well as for male and female youth.

- Youth sharing tents must be no more than two years apart in age.

- In Cub Scouting, parents and guardians may share a tent with their family.

- In all other programs, youth and adults tent separately.

- Spouses may share tents.

Lodging/Cabin Accommodations

Whenever possible, separate cabins or lodging should be provided for male and female adults as well as for male and female youth. Where separate accommodations cannot be provided due to group size or limited availability, modifications may be made. Where completely separate accommodations are not available, additional supervision is required.

- If adults and youth of the same gender occupy single-room accommodations, there must be a minimum of two adults and four youth, with all adults being Youth Protection trained.

- Physical separation by other means, including temporary barriers or space, should be used only when no other arrangements are possible.

- These modifications are limited to single-gender accommodations.

Restrooms

Separate shower and latrine facilities should be provided for male and female adults as well as for male and female youth. If separate facilities are not available, separate times should be scheduled and posted.

Privacy of youth is respected.

- Adults and youth must respect each other's privacy, especially in situations such as changing clothes and taking showers at camp.

- Adult leaders should closely monitor these areas but only enter as needed for youth protection or health and safety reasons.

Program Requirements

The buddy system should be used.

The use of smartphones, cameras, mirrors, drones, etc., in places or situations where privacy is expected is prohibited.

All aspects of the Scouting program are open to observation by parents and leaders.

The BSA does not recognize any secret organizations as part of its program.

Hazing and initiations are prohibited and have no part during any Scouting activity.

All forms of bullying and harassment including verbal, physical, and cyberbullying are prohibited.

Inappropriate public displays of affection are prohibited.

Sexual activity is prohibited.

Appropriate attire is required for all activities.

Reporting Requirements

Adult leaders and youth members have a responsibility to recognize, respond to, and report Youth Protection violations and abuse.

Mandatory Report of Child Abuse

If you see or suspect a child is being abused, stop the abuse immediately and report it. All persons involved in BSA programs must report any instance of child abuse to local law enforcement and, in some states, also to the state's child protective services, or CPS. This includes any good-faith suspicion or belief that a child is or has been physically or sexually abused, physically or emotionally neglected, exposed to any form of violence or threat, or exposed to any form of sexual exploitation including the possession, manufacture, or distribution of sexually exploitive images, online solicitation, enticement, or showing of obscene material.

This duty cannot be delegated to any other person. After reporting to law enforcement, the matter must also be reported to the Scout executive so appropriate actions may be taken. If unable to reach the Scout executive, contact the Scouts First Helpline at 1-844-SCOUTS1 (1-844-726-8871).

Ensure notification has been made to parents/guardian. Failing to report suspected child abuse may be a criminal law violation in your state. It is important to note that all states allow immunity from criminal and civil liability for good-faith reporting of suspected abuse, even if it is later determined to be unfounded.

Fore more information, please see your state's reporting statutes on the Child Welfare Information Gateway website at www.childwelfare.gov.

Additional BSA Reporting

Youth Protection Policy Violations

- Serious Youth Protection policy violations or behaviors that put a youth's safety at risk must be reported to the local council Scout executive.

- Alternatively, policy violations may be reported to the Scouts First Helpline when the local council Scout executive is not available.

- Online reporting is also available at www.scouting.org/health-and-safety/incident-report.

Speaking With a Child Who Discloses or Indicates Abuse

When speaking with a child who discloses or indicates abuse, your role is to become the *trusted adult*. A trusted adult is someone with whom a child can talk freely about their feelings and problems and who provides healthy guidance and support.

When informed about abuse, a trusted adult

- Gets actively involved.

- Sees something and stops it.

- Suspects something and reports it.

Seek advice from an expert when you are unsure.

Adults should recognize that talking with children about abuse, especially sexual abuse, is not comfortable for anyone; however, a child's first time telling someone—and your response—may have lasting effects. If a child reports that they have been abused, it is important that you listen to all that they have to say. Then, respond calmly and support the child through the reporting process. Tell the child it wasn't their fault and express belief in the child's disclosure by simply stating, "I believe you." This will further support and validate the child's statement. You do not need details from the child. However, you should get the following information:

- Name and address of the child alleging abuse, if known

- Name and address of the alleged offender, if known

- Location of the alleged abuse

- Nature (e.g., sexual, physical, emotional) and extent of the alleged abuse

- Approximate date of the last incident (if an older child)

Parents Reporting Violations of BSA Youth Protection Policies

If an adult leader or someone else in Scouting is trying to convince your child that their advancements or awards are solely dependent on that person's approval, or if that person is asking your child to do anything that seems inappropriate, contact your local council Scout executive immediately.

EXERCISES ON PERSONAL SAFETY AWARENESS

Now that you understand the types of abuse, the barriers that we have put in place to minimize abuse, and the steps to take when you suspect abuse has occurred, let's focus on helping you empower your child. Concerned and connected parents and caregivers are a strong component of all child abuse prevention strategies. You have an important role to play in prevention!

Many parents find it difficult to talk with their child about abuse. However, it is important to provide a foundation for a child to understand personal safety and encourage them to come to you with questions and concerns. The personal safety exercises in this section, to be used in conversations with your child, will help you with this process. They focus on five very important areas that can minimize the chances of abuse for your child:

- Why should I check with a parent first?

- Who are my *trusted adults*?

- What are my personal boundaries?

- What if someone asks me to keep a secret?

- How do I talk about touches and private parts?

Five Topics to Cover With Children

NOTE: Completing the exercises described in these pages fulfills the requirements for your Cub Scout to earn their badge or rank and must be completed for each rank earned. The BSA recommends that these exercises be conducted on a regular basis throughout the year.

Why should I check with a parent first?

Many abusers are known to the child as a family friend, relative, Scouter, or older youth, so it is important to focus safety messages on the behavior of a person, not the relationship to the child. Teach your child to check with you first before agreeing to go anywhere with another person. Tell your child never to go anywhere with anyone who will not let them check with you first. If the person refuses, your child has the right to step back from the person, make noise, say "No," run away, and tell someone.

Tell your child that your permission is required before they may accept an invitation from a Scout leader or another parent to an activity outside of Scouting and that all such invitations must be reported to you. The BSA recommends that parents not allow one-on-one contact and insist that two adults are present (two-deep leadership) at any Scouting activities for their children.

Try this exercise to help your child remember to check first. Brainstorm times and situations in which your child should always come to you before going somewhere with someone. Include such situations as going into a house or vehicle, changing plans, being offered gifts, and being asked for help.

Talk through and role-play the following scenarios:

"What if a neighbor asks you to come into his house to see his new puppy?" *I would tell him that I need to check with you first. I would come home and check first before I went over to their house.* Ask the child about other responses.

"What if you are playing in the park and a nice person asks you to come to a different part of the park to help him or her find something they lost?" *I need to check first before changing my plans so that my parents know where I am.* Ask the child what other ways they could respond.

"What if an older youth friend of your brother is spending the night and wakes you up to sneak outside?" *I also need to check first before helping an adult or teenager. Adults and teenagers usually ask other adults for help. I can help if I check first and you come with me to ask my parents for permission.*

What are my personal boundaries?

Try this exercise to help your child learn to create and maintain personal boundaries that make them feel safe. This exercise is designed to empower kids to tell people that they are uncomfortable and want another person to leave their personal space immediately. Discuss what private parts are and where they are located. Lessons on personal boundaries should begin early in a child's development and should cover belongings, emotions, and their body. Focus on asking permission and receiving consent. Tell your child that any time someone touches them in a way that they do not want to be touched, they have your permission to take some big steps back and say "NO," and then go tell a *trusted adult* what happened. Explain that stepping back can give them room to think and move. Then have your child practice taking big steps away from a person and saying "NO" in a firm voice. Explain to the child that regardless of what the adult or teenager says—or what your child was doing or has done—you will believe and protect them.

Talk through the following scenarios. Ask them how they could use "NO" to create space for themselves in these situations.

"What if someone drives up, gets out of their car, and starts walking toward you to ask you for directions?"

"What if another kid your age continues to hug you even though you have asked them to stop?"

"What if you are spending the night or on a campout and someone touches your body while you are sleeping?"

How do I talk about touches and private parts?

Young people should be told that the parts of their body covered by their swimsuit are their private parts, and they have the right to say no to being touched there. Body parts should be called by their appropriate names to assist in developing a healthy and positive body image. Encourage your child to say no and then tell you if someone tries to touch or look at the child's private parts, or wants your child to touch or look at their private parts.

It is important to remind children that if they get tricked into a scary or confusing touch or if they freeze and are unable to say no, it is OK and not their fault. Children should be encouraged to tell as soon as they feel comfortable doing so. Keep the lines of communication open by reminding them that they can talk to you about touches, even a long time after something happened.

Try this exercise to help your child resist someone who is trying to touch their private parts. Pose these scenarios, and then discuss the solutions.

"What if your friend's babysitter or another youth asks you to wrestle without clothes on?"

"What if that same friend asks you to keep the touching games secret?"

"What if your Scout leader touches your private parts or shows you their private parts?"

For more information, see "Hot Chocolate Talk" under "National Resources."

Who are my trusted adults?

Young people should have at least five adults you have identified with whom they can talk freely about their feelings and problems and who provide healthy attention and affection. A child who has such a network of *trusted adults* will be more difficult for an adult who abuses children to groom. The list of five adults might change depending on the child's circumstances. Prior to Scouting or other activities, parents should discuss with their child who they will turn to if someone is violating a rule or making them uncomfortable.

Try this exercise to help your child identify trusted adults. Explain that a trusted adult is someone the child knows well who is willing to listen and offer advice when needed. Trace your child's hand on a piece of paper. Ask your child to write or draw a person on each finger that they can go to for help or advice. Help your child determine the trusted adults. Explain that if a situation occurs where a trusted adult is needed, your child needs to remember this list. And if one of the people on the list cannot help, or is the one causing the problem, your child should go to another person on the list. Remind them that they can also say "NO" if a trusted adult is making them feel uneasy or uncomfortable.

> Ask your child these questions, making sure the options are understood. Ask who their trusted adult would be and how they could talk to them about what happened.
>
> "What if something happens on a camping trip (or at a neighbor's house, or at a friend's house) that makes you feel afraid or confused?"
>
> "What if someone is making you feel uneasy or uncomfortable, and the first person you tell can't, doesn't, or won't help you?"
>
> "What if one of your *trusted adults* is making you feel unsafe or uncomfortable?"

What if someone asks me to keep a secret?

Adults who abuse children often try to groom children by convincing them to keep secrets about activities that they would not want their parents to know about (drinking, smoking, pornography, etc.). A child wanting to keep those activities secret might also see any abuse as something to keep secret. Your child must feel like they can come to you and be heard about little concerns as well as big problems. Tell your child it is not OK for people to ask them to keep a secret from you or another caregiver. Give your child a simple, automatic solution. Let your child know that they can come to you about anything and that you will still love and support them.

Try this exercise to help your child understand the difference between *secrets* and *surprises*. Tell your child that a secret is something that is hidden from others. A surprise is something that we keep quiet about for a short period of time and then everyone finds out together, like what you bought someone for their birthday. Surprises are usually OK, but secrets can be harmful if they cover up something unsafe or scary. Say that if your child is not sure whether something is a secret or a surprise, they can always ask you or a trusted adult.

> Ask your child what to do in the following situations. Ask them how they could determine whether this is a surprise or a secret.
>
> "What if a bigger kid says he will give you $20 if you play a secret touching game with him?"
>
> "What if an adult says that you don't need to bring a buddy because they have a surprise that is just for you?"
>
> "What if someone you know asks if he can email you a secret picture or asks you to pose for naughty pictures?"

For additional information, please see the BSA's Cyber Chip tool and resources at www.scouting.org/training/youth-protection/cyber-chip and the NetSmartz Scouting Portal at www.netsmartz.org/scouting/.

Putting It Together

Reviewing these five personal safety rules and allowing your child to design their own "What If" games can help make personal safety awareness less scary and more accessible for your child and the whole family. The most important points to make sure your child knows are as follows:

- Check with a parent first.

- Have a buddy with you at all times.

- Maintain your personal space.

- Avoid secrets.

- Know who your *trusted adults* are.

> Consider having a "Family Safety Night" at the beginning and the end of every school year or new activity. Reviewing rules about bike helmets, fire escape plans, and calling 911 should lead into conversations about abuse, bullying, personal safety awareness, and online safety so that they can be treated like any other concern.

The BSA's Youth Protection program is based on

- Parental involvement

- Chartered organizations

- Leader selection and monitoring

- Each leader's knowledge of and adherence to BSA Youth Protection and Health and Safety policies

- Commitment of all adults to the safety of youth

- Recognizing, responding, and reporting

- Youth Protection Begins With YOU

ADDITIONAL BSA RESOURCES

Youth Protection webpage:
www.scouting.org/training/youth-protection

Youth Protection Training: https://my.scouting.org

Youth Protection policies and Health and Safety procedures continue to be updated regularly. For the most up-to-date information and changes or additions to policies and procedures, go to www.scouting.org/health-and-safety/gss.

Guide to Safe Scouting: www.scouting.org/health-and-safety/gss

Scouts First Helpline: 1-844-SCOUTS1 (1-844-726-8871)

BSA Member Care: 972-580-2489

Scouter Code of Conduct: https://filestore.scouting.org/filestore/HealthSafety/pdf/Scouter_Code_of_Conduct.pdf

BSA incident reporting:
www.scouting.org/health-and-safety/incident-report

State-by-state mandatory reporting information:
www.childwelfare.gov

NATIONAL RESOURCES

National Center for Missing and Exploited Children—information on digital/online safety and reporting

Netsmartz: www.netsmartz.org.

CyberTipline: 800-843-5678

www.childhelp.org: 800-4-A-Child (800-422-4453)

www.preventchildabuse.gov

Committee for Children: www.cfchildren.org

Hot Chocolate Talk: www.cfchildren.org/blog/2018/03/the-hot-chocolate-talk/

www.stopbullying.gov

www.suicidepreventionlifeline.org: 800-273-8255

NOTES

NOTES

NOTES

NOTES

Prepared. For Life.®

BOY SCOUTS OF AMERICA
1325 West Walnut Hill Lane
P.O. Box 152079
Irving, Texas 75015-2079
www.scouting.org

100-0
2018 Print

WELCOME TO THE
BEAR
HANDBOOK

Being a Bear Scout means enjoying awesome adventures.

Have a great year!

34753
ISBN 978-0-8395-0111-4
©2018 Boy Scouts of America
2018 Printing

Table of Contents

BEAR ELECTIVE ADVENTURES

Welcome, Bear!

Welcome to a fun and exciting year of Cub Scouting, Bear! You'll go on adventures, exploring the world around you with other Bears in your den. You will play games, make fun things, learn about wildlife, and spend time outdoors. You'll even earn awards while having all this fun!

Your Bear Den

As a Bear in the Boy Scouts of America, you belong to a den of kids who are Bears just like you! They are in your grade or are the same age as you, and it will be fun to explore Bear adventures with them at den meetings.

Your Bear Pack

You, your family, and your den go to a monthly pack meeting, where everyone in all the dens in the pack get together at the same time. It's a chance to enjoy interesting programs and also a time for awards.

Cub Scouting and *The Jungle Book*

Great Britain's Lord Baden-Powell started worldwide Scouting in 1907, and the Boy Scouts of America began in 1910. Lord Baden-Powell really liked the stories in *The Jungle Book* by Rudyard Kipling. When Cub Scouting started in 1930, names and ideas were borrowed from *The Jungle Book* to make the program fun and exciting.

Maybe you know about Baloo the bear, who helps teach the child Mowgli (MO-glee) the laws of the jungle so he can live among the animals. Lord Baden-Powell knew it was important to have a wise leader like Akela (Ah-KAY-la), the wolf. Akela lets the child Mowgli join the wolf pack.

To this day, we have names like Akela and Baloo and words like den and pack in Cub Scouting. That's our way of remembering how Cub Scouting began with *The Jungle Book*.

Bear Leaders

As a Bear Scout, you have several people you can call "Akela" like the wise leader in *The Jungle Book*. These include the den leader, the assistant den leader, and your parent or guardian. Akela can be anyone who is older than you and a wise teacher.

These leaders help you to learn new things, and they can even help you find new ways to use what you have already learned!

Did you know you can help lead your den by becoming a denner? The denner is a Scout chosen to help Akela at meetings and outings. If you're selected to be the denner, **do your best!**

Remember that **"Do your best!"** is the Cub Scout motto.

Note to Parents and Other Caring Adults

It's important to Scouting that every pack and den have great adult leadership. Packs are led by a Cubmaster and pack committee, while dens are guided by den leaders.

Parents help with den and pack activities and are encouraged to take training to prepare to become part of Cub Scout volunteer leadership. All adults who work directly with youth are required to take Youth Protection training.

Your Bear Uniform

Your uniform is an important part of being a Cub Scout. Wearing it lets people know that you belong to a Bear den and a pack and, most important, you belong to the Boy Scouts of America! You should wear the uniform to den meetings, pack meetings, and any special activities you participate in as a Bear.

The official uniform for Cub Scouts includes blue Cub Scout pants or shorts and shirt with insignia for your rank. Each rank has its own neckerchief and slide in the rank colors and a belt buckle to be worn with the blue Cub Scout belt. Bear Scouts can also wear an official navy-blue cap with a light blue front panel and Bear emblem.

Wearing the Cub Scout uniform shows you are a member of the team.

The pictures on the next page show you where to put the Bear Scout insignia on the sleeves and pockets of your uniform.

You might receive a patch for participating in day camp or a council popcorn sale. This is an example of "temporary insignia" and should be worn centered on the right pocket.

While serving as a denner, you will wear gold shoulder cords suspended from the left shoulder of your uniform.

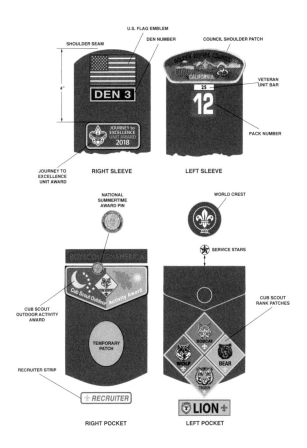

U.S. FLAG EMBLEM
SHOULDER SEAM
DEN NUMBER
COUNCIL SHOULDER PATCH

DEN 3

JOURNEY to EXCELLENCE UNIT AWARD 2018

VETERAN UNIT BAR

PACK NUMBER

JOURNEY TO EXCELLENCE UNIT AWARD

RIGHT SLEEVE

LEFT SLEEVE

NATIONAL SUMMERTIME AWARD PIN

WORLD CREST

SERVICE STARS

CUB SCOUT OUTDOOR ACTIVITY AWARD

CUB SCOUT RANK PATCHES

BOBCAT
WOLF
BEAR
TIGER

TEMPORARY PATCH

RECRUITER STRIP

RECRUITER

LION

RIGHT POCKET

LEFT POCKET

Bear Adventures

The Cub Scout activities that you do with your den and family this year are called Bear adventures. You'll have fun meeting the requirements with the help of your den leaders and other caring adults. Some of the adventures are ones that all Bears will do, and others will be ones that you and your den choose.

When you have completed each required adventure and selected elective adventure, your den leader will give approval by signing your handbook. Once you have met all requirements, you will earn the rank of Bear.

Character Compass

As you work on your Bear adventures in this *Bear Handbook*, you will notice this symbol:

A compass is a tool that guides a person from place to place. Character is how we act, and it guides our entire lives. This compass will be your guide to one or more of the 12 points of the Scout Law. It will help you think about how the points of the Scout Law guide our way in Cub Scouting and in daily life. The 12 points are all different, and each one is a treasure for you to find.

We know that you want your Bear Scout to grow up to be self-reliant, dependable, and caring. And we know that you want to teach your child to "do your best" every day. Scouting has the same goals in mind for each young person.

The mission of the Boy Scouts of America is to prepare young people to make ethical and moral choices over their lifetimes by instilling in them the values of the Scout Oath and Scout Law.

Scouts are guided by the Scout Oath and Scout Law. These are printed on the back cover of this book.

The Scout Oath and the Scout Law are defined as part of the Bobcat requirements in the next section of this handbook. You may find it helpful to review these explanations with your Scout from time to time.

Please note also that the Boy Scouts of America has always held steadfastly to the principle, embodied in the Scout Oath, that a Scout has a duty to God. The BSA does not promote any specific religion and is completely nonsectarian.

THE OUTDOOR CODE

Much of Scouting, including Cub Scouting, happens outside. For more than 60 years, the Outdoor Code has been a guide for Scouts in the outdoors. Remember to do your best by showing respect for the outdoors and by learning and upholding the Outdoor Code.

THE OUTDOOR CODE

As an American, I will do my best to—

* Be clean in my outdoor manners,
* Be careful with fire,
* Be considerate in the outdoors, and
* Be conservation-minded.

Being clean in your outdoor manners, careful with fire, and considerate means you can enjoy the outdoors in ways that do no harm to the environment. Being conservation-minded encourages the protection and thoughtful use of natural resources and doing your part to improve the condition of the land and the environment.

As a Cub Scout, you will learn to use the Leave No Trace Principles for Kids to help you take care of an area where you hike or camp.

LEAVE NO TRACE PRINCIPLES FOR KIDS*

Center for Outdoor Ethics | LNT.org

1. Know Before You Go. Find out about the place you're going to camp ahead of time. Are there rules you need to know about? Are any activities against the rules? Is water available? Do you need to bring anything special?

2. Choose the Right Path. Always walk on trails, even if that means getting your boots muddy. Don't take shortcuts. Set up tents in marked camping areas.

3. Trash Your Trash. Use bathroom facilities when available. Follow campground rules for handling dishwater. Pack out all your trash unless the campground has trash pickup.

4. Leave What You Find. Leave any natural treasures where you find them so other campers can enjoy them, too. If you want a souvenir of your campout, take a picture. A good saying to remember is "Leave nothing but footprints, take nothing but pictures, kill nothing but time."

5. Be Careful With Fire. Cook on a camp stove or grill whenever possible. It's easier and less messy than cooking over an open fire. Only build fires in designated fire rings. Always have someone keep an eye on your fire until it is dead out.

6. Respect Wildlife. Travel quietly and give animals enough space that you don't disturb them. Getting too close to an animal can potentially hurt the animal and you. Take pictures from a safe distance. You're visiting the animal's home, so be considerate.

7. Be Kind to Other Visitors. Be respectful of other visitors by keeping noise down and not entering other groups' campsites without permission. Be polite to other people you meet. Give them the respect you expect from them.

To help you remember the Outdoor Code and the Leave No Trace Principles for Kids, you can find them in the back of your handbook.

*The member-driven Leave No Trace Center for Outdoor Ethics teaches people how to enjoy the outdoors responsibly. This copyrighted information has been reprinted with permission from the Leave No Trace Center for Outdoor Ethics: www.LNT.org.

Bobcat!

If you haven't already earned your Bobcat badge, you will need to start your Cub Scouting adventures by learning what it takes to become a Bobcat.

Read through the Bobcat requirements and practice several times what you have learned. When you think that you are ready, share what you've learned with your family and your den. Then give yourself a pat on the back and congratulate yourself on earning your Bobcat badge.

BOBCAT REQUIREMENTS

1. Learn and say the Scout Oath, with help if needed.
2. Learn and say the Scout Law, with help if needed.
3. Show the Cub Scout sign. Tell what it means.
4. Show the Cub Scout handshake. Tell what it means.
5. Say the Cub Scout motto. Tell what it means.
6. Show the Cub Scout salute. Tell what it means.
7. With your parent or guardian, complete the exercises in the pamphlet *How to Protect Your Children From Child Abuse: A Parent's Guide.*

1 | Learn and say the Scout Oath, with help if needed.

One of the most important parts of that is to understand that all members of the Boy Scouts of America believe in, live by, and often repeat the Scout Oath and the Scout Law. We learn those words and believe in them as a way to live our lives and be good members of our families, our communities, and the Boy Scouts of America!

Scout Oath

On my honor I will do my best
To do my duty to God and my country
and to obey the Scout Law;
To help other people at all times;
To keep myself physically strong,
mentally awake, and morally straight.

The Meaning of the Scout Oath

ON MY HONOR ...

Saying "On my honor" is like saying "I promise."

I WILL DO MY BEST ...

This means that you will do your best to do what the Scout Oath says.

The Scout Oath has several parts.
Let's look at what they mean.

TO DO MY DUTY ... A duty is something you are expected to do. At home, you might be expected to make up your bed or take out the trash. You also have duties to God and to your country.

TO GOD ... You do your duty to God by following the teachings of your family and religious leaders.

AND MY COUNTRY ... You do your duty to your country by being a good citizen and obeying the law.

AND TO OBEY THE SCOUT LAW; ... You also promise to live by the 12 points of the Scout Law, which are described on the next page.

TO HELP OTHER PEOPLE AT ALL TIMES; ... Many people need help. A friendly smile and a helping hand make life easier for others. By helping other people, you are doing a Good Turn and making our world a better place.

TO KEEP MYSELF PHYSICALLY STRONG, ... This part of the Scout Oath is about taking care of yourself. You stay physically strong when you eat the right foods and get plenty of exercise.

MENTALLY AWAKE, ... You stay mentally awake when you work hard in school, learn all you can, and ask questions.

AND MORALLY STRAIGHT. You stay morally straight when you do the right thing and live your life with honesty.

_____   _____
Date   **Den Leader's OK**

Scout Law

A Scout is trustworthy, loyal, helpful, friendly, courteous, kind, obedient, cheerful, thrifty, brave, clean, and reverent.

The Meaning of the Scout Law

The Scout Law has 12 points. Each is a goal for every Scout. A Scout tries to live up to the Law every day. It is not always easy to do, but a Scout always tries.

A Scout is TRUSTWORTHY. Tell the truth and keep your promises. People can depend on you.

A Scout is LOYAL. Be true to your family, friends, Scout leaders, school, and country.

A Scout is HELPFUL. Volunteer to help others without expecting a reward.

A Scout is FRIENDLY. Be a friend to everyone, even people who are very different from you.

A Scout is COURTEOUS. Be polite to everyone and always use good manners.

A Scout is KIND. Treat others as you want to be treated. Never harm or kill any living thing without good reason.

A Scout is OBEDIENT. Follow the rules of your family, school, and pack. Obey the laws of your community and country.

A Scout is CHEERFUL. Look for the bright side of life. Cheerfully do tasks that come your way. Try to make others happy.

A Scout is THRIFTY. Work to pay your own way. Don't be wasteful. Use time, property, and natural resources wisely.

A Scout is BRAVE. Face difficult situations even when you feel afraid. Do what is right despite what others might be doing or saying.

A Scout is CLEAN. Keep your body and mind fit. Help keep your home and community clean.

A Scout is REVERENT. Be reverent toward God. Be faithful in your religious duties. Respect the beliefs of others.

_____   _____
Date   **Den Leader's OK**

3 | Show the Cub Scout sign. Tell what it means.

Make the sign with your right hand. Hold your arm straight up. The two raised fingers stand for the Scout Oath and the Scout Law. The fingers look like the sharp ears of the wolf ready to listen to Akela! Remember that Akela means "good leader" to a Cub Scout. Your mother or father or guardian is Akela. So is your Cubmaster or your den leader. At school, your teacher is Akela.

_____   _____
Date   **Den Leader's OK**

4 | Show the Cub Scout handshake. Tell what it means.

When you shake hands with another Cub Scout, do this: Hold out your right hand just as you always do to shake hands. But then put your first two fingers along the inside of the other Scout's wrist. This means that you help each other to remember and obey the Scout Oath and Scout Law.

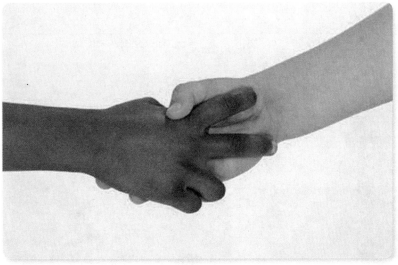

_____   _____
Date   Den Leader's OK

The Cub Scout motto is "Do Your Best."

A motto is a guiding principle and a rule for living. Do Your Best means trying your hardest, not just a little bit. Do your best all the time. Do your best in school and at home. Do your best when you play a game and help your team. Do your best as you work on your rank adventures!

_____   _____
Date   Den Leader's OK

Salute with your right hand. Hold your first two fingers close together. Touch your fingertips to your cap. If you aren't wearing a cap, touch your right eyebrow.

You salute the flag to show respect to our country. Always use the Cub Scout salute when you are in your Cub Scout uniform, both indoors and outdoors. If you are not in uniform, you salute the flag by placing your right hand over your heart.

_____   _____
Date   **Den Leader's OK**

7 | **With your parent or guardian, complete the exercises in the pamphlet *How to Protect Your Children From Child Abuse: A Parent's Guide.***

If your handbook does not include the pamphlet, talk with your den leader.

_____   _____
Date   **Den Leader's OK**

Congratulations on earning your Bobcat badge! You may now continue on the trail of your Bear adventures! Let's take a look at what those adventures are called, what you need to do to earn your Bear badge, and all the fun things you will explore as a Bear.

The Bear Adventures and Requirements

BEAR BADGE REQUIREMENTS

Note to Parents and Other Caring Adults

Requirements do not need to be completed in any particular order. In developing the plan for the order in which to do the Bear adventures, den leaders will look at many factors, including seasonal considerations. Note that both Bear Necessities and Fur, Feathers, and Ferns include activities to be done in the out-of-doors.

1. Complete each of the six required adventures.

 Baloo the Builder

 Bear Claws

 *Bear Necessities

 Fellowship and Duty to God

 *Fur, Feathers, and Ferns

 Paws for Action (Duty to Country)

*Seasonal considerations

2. In addition to the six required adventures listed previously, complete at least one elective adventure of your den's or family's choosing.

BEAR ELECTIVE ADVENTURES

 A Bear Goes Fishing

 Marble Madness

 Bear Picnic Basket

 Roaring Laughter

 Beat of the Drum

 Robotics

 Critter Care

 Salmon Run

 Forensics

 Super Science

 Grin and Bear It

 A World of Sound

 Make It Move

3. With your parent, guardian, or other caring adult, complete the exercises in the pamphlet *How to Protect Your Children From Child Abuse: A Parent's Guide.*

4. Earn the Cyber Chip award for your age. (The Cyber Chip portion of this requirement may be waived by your parent or guardian if you do not have access to the internet.)

Once you have achieved all of the Bear rank badge requirements and your handbook has been signed, you are ready to earn your Bear badge!

Let out a big GRAND HOWL, Bear Scout!

BALOO THE BUILDER

REQUIRED ADVENTURE

Complete all of the following requirements.

1. Discover which hand tools are the best ones to have in your toolbox. Learn the rules for using these tools safely. Practice with at least four of these tools before beginning a project.

2. Select, plan, and define the materials for the project you will complete in requirement 3.

3. Assemble your materials, and build one useful project and one fun project using wood.

4. Apply a finish to one of your projects.

SNAPSHOT OF ADVENTURE

Learning to build things that are useful or fun is an important skill. You might grow up to build houses as a career or models as a hobby. Or you might just learn some skills that will help you in everyday life.

Building materials may include wood, cement, plastic, steel, or a combination of all these things. For this adventure, we will focus on wood. You will learn about hand tools and how to use them safely. You will learn how to choose the right type of wood for a project and follow project instructions. And before you are finished, you will use your new skills to make two projects from wood.

COMPLETE ALL OF THE FOLLOWING REQUIREMENTS.

REQUIREMENT 1 | **Discover which hand tools are the best ones to have in your toolbox. Learn the rules for using these tools safely. Practice with at least four of these tools before beginning a project.**

Note to Parents and Other Caring Adults

Cub Scouts are not allowed to use power tools. Safety is the primary concern as Bear Scouts learn to use woodworking tools.

A woodworker may have dozens—or even hundreds—of tools. You will only need a few tools to complete this adventure.

Using the right tool for the right job is very important. This keeps your tools in good working order. It also keeps you safe. It is a good idea to inspect your tools before using them to be certain they are in good condition.

A Scout is trustworthy. Show that you can be trusted to use tools by following safety rules.

Here are some tools you might want in your toolbox. You may borrow these tools from your parent, neighbor, or den leader, but always ask permission first.

When you have finished learning about these tools and how to use them safely, practice using them on pieces of scrap wood.

SAFETY GLASSES

Safety glasses aren't really tools, but they can help keep you safe when you are using tools. It is extremely important that you protect your eyes when working with tools and wood. You will need a good pair of safety glasses that are kid-sized.

Safety glasses are different from regular glasses or sunglasses. They are designed not to break when something hits them. They also cover a larger area around your eyes to keep sawdust and other construction debris out. Keep them clean with a soft cloth, and store them in a safe spot. Wearing safety glasses while working is like wearing your safety belt in a car. Don't think about it. Just do it!

HAMMER

A hammer is used to drive nails into wood. There are many different kinds of hammers. The best one for a Cub Scout is an 8- to 10-ounce claw hammer like the one shown here.

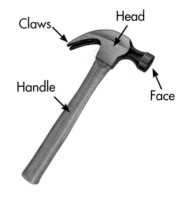

Claws   Head

Handle   Face

To drive a nail, hold it in place with one hand and tap it in gently with the hammer in your other hand. When the nail stands by itself, move your hand out of the way, and give the nail several firm hits with the hammer. For the most force, hold the handle near the end, not near the head.

If a nail bends, pull it out with the hammer's claws. Set a small block of wood next to the nail. Place the head of the hammer on the block of wood, and slide the claws under the head of the nail. That creates a lever that helps you easily pull the nail out. Start over with a new nail.

 Safety: Do not use a hammer that is too large or heavy for you. Grip the hammer tightly so it does not slip from your hand. Be careful of the fingers on your other hand. If they get in the way, it will hurt!

SCREWDRIVER

A screwdriver puts a screw into a piece of wood. Screws do a better job than nails of holding projects together when the pieces will be under strain.

There are two main kinds of screwdrivers: slotted and Phillips. Pick the one with a tip that matches the screw you want to drive. A slotted screw has a single slot across its head. A Phillips screw has an "X" design.

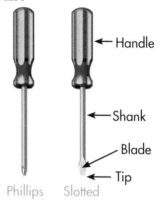

← Handle

←Shank

Blade

← Tip

Phillips   Slotted

Screws go in more easily if you first make a pilot hole with a brace and bit (see the following page). The pilot hole should be smaller in diameter than the screw. It can also help to rub a little soap on the threads, or ridges, of the screw.

Safety: Use the longest screwdriver you can handle that is practical for your job. Pick the screwdriver that best fits the screws you are using. Only use a screwdriver to drive screws.

BRACE AND BIT

A brace and bit is used to drill holes. This is a two-part tool. The bit does the drilling, and the brace turns the bit. There are many kinds and sizes of bits depending on the material and size of hole needed. All bits for wood have a spiral edge that digs out small pieces of wood as you turn it.

The brace has a hole where you insert the bit. Tighten the chuck so the bit is held firmly in place while you are working with it.

Head →
Handle →
Chuck →
Bit →

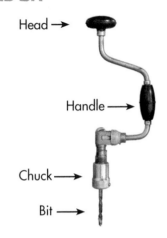

To use the tool, guide the bit into place with one hand. Press down firmly with one hand on the head to keep the bit in place. Turn the handle clockwise with your other hand to drill your hole.

Before you drill all the way through the wood, turn the wood over, and finish your hole from the other side. This step will keep the wood from splintering.

 Safety: The bit has a sharp point, so be careful when handling it. Use two hands. You may need an adult's help to get the hole started. Put on safety glasses before you begin.

HAND SAW

A hand saw lets you cut boards along straight lines. A 20-inch hand saw is best for Scouts your age.

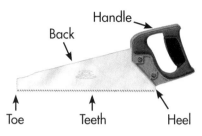

Handle

Back

Toe   Teeth   Heel

Before you begin sawing, draw a pencil mark on the board where you want to make your cut. Start the cut by making a notch on the mark at the edge of the board. This notch will act as a track for the blade to sit in. Steady the blade with your thumb well above the cutting edge, and then draw back gently to create the notch.

Now, remove your thumb, and begin sawing down the pencil mark. Be sure to tilt the saw at a 45-degree angle to the board. Cutting the wood is a simple action of pushing the saw away from you at a downward angle, then pulling it back toward you. Each time you do this, the sharp teeth of the saw will cut deeper into the wood. You may need to straighten the saw handle to correct the direction of the cut, but be careful not to pinch the saw. If this happens, gently work the saw back and forth to release the blade.

 Safety: A saw has sharp teeth. Be careful when you carry it and when you lay it down. It is a good idea to keep your saw hanging up when not in use so you don't brush up against the teeth. Always know where all your fingers are when using a saw. This tool will create sawdust, so safety glasses are a must.

COPING SAW

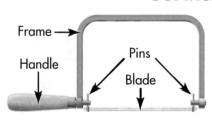

A coping saw lets you cut curves and odd shapes in wood. Hold the wood securely with a vise or C-clamp (see below) so it can't move. Mark the curve you want to cut, then follow it with the saw, making long back-and-forth strokes. A heavy blade is a good idea.

 Safety: Like a hand saw, a coping saw has lots of sharp teeth. Be careful with your fingers, and wear safety glasses.

VISE OR CLAMP

At times, you may feel like you need a third hand to hold the wood you are cutting or drilling. Using a vise or clamp is like having that third hand. To use a vise or clamp, place the wood between the jaws, then tighten the tension bar to hold the wood in place.

 Safety: Vises and clamps can pinch fingers and hands, so be careful as you tighten them. If you are using a vise, make sure it is properly secured to a table.

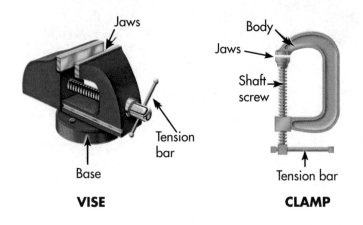

VISE

CLAMP

MEASURING DEVICE

Carpenters have a favorite saying: "Measure twice and cut once." To measure things you are cutting, you can use a measuring tape, a ruler, or a speed square. A speed square rests on the straight edge of a board to help you mark a straight line across it. A measuring tape or ruler lets you measure the length of a board you want to cut.

SANDPAPER

Sandpaper is just what it sounds like: a piece of heavy-duty paper that has a scratchy surface on one side. Sandpaper is used to rub off any rough edges on your project. It comes in grades ranging from very coarse (very scratchy) to very fine (not very scratchy). Most of the time,

you will shape the wood with a coarse sandpaper first. Then change to a finer sandpaper to make a smooth surface.

You can make a hand sander by nailing or gluing a piece of sandpaper around a wooden block you can hold in your hand. Home improvement stores also sell hand sanders.

SMALL FIRST-AID KIT

When working with tools, it is always a good idea to have a small first-aid kit nearby. It should include adhesive bandages in case you cut yourself, tweezers, a small magnifying glass, and some antiseptic, in case you get a splinter.

PRACTICING WITH TOOLS

Here are some ways you can practice using your tools:

♦ With a hammer, see how many hits it takes you to drive a nail into a piece of wood, or see how many nails you can drive in five minutes.

♦ With a screwdriver, see how long it takes you to place one screw through two small pieces of wood. You could also use a vise or a clamp with this, which is using two tools at one time.

♦ With a saw, see how well you cut using different thicknesses of wood. Check your cuts to make sure they are straight down, not slanted.

I practiced using the following tools:

1. _____

2. _____

3. _____

4. _____

Once you have finished with your tools, wipe them off with an old cloth or rag—being careful not to touch blades or sharp edges—and place them back where they belong. This will help your tools last longer. It will also help you find them the next time you need them.

_____   _____
Date   **Den Leader's OK**

A Scout is helpful. Working with tools can be messy. If you notice safe ways you can help clean up, offer to help!

You can use the tools you've learned about to make many kinds of projects, but all of them will begin with similar steps. Here's how to plan a project and read instructions or drawings.

1. Select your project. Will it be something useful, something fun to play with, or a gift for another person?

2. Read the directions. If you are using project instructions or drawings, read through them completely before beginning. Then read them one more time.

Just as a road map shows the route from one place to another, project instructions or drawings show you how to complete your project from beginning to end. It is important to read through the instructions before you begin to gather your materials. They may tell you the best type of wood for the project, how thick it should be, and how much you will need. You might also need other items, such as nails, screws, glue, and paint. You will also be able to determine which tools you will need.

The next page includes the instructions for a simple tic-tac-toe board. As you can see, the picture only shows the finished result. It does not show any dimensions or other details.

Later in this adventure, you will find more detailed instructions for other projects. Compare those instructions with the tic-tac-toe instructions. Which one helps you understand how to build your project in a better way? How could it be helpful to have both kinds of instructions (written and illustrated)?

TIC-TAC-TOE BOARD

Cut a block of wood so it is 4 inches by 4 inches by 1 inch. Mark evenly spaced holes, and drill. Paint golf tees—five of one color for "X" and five of another color for "O."

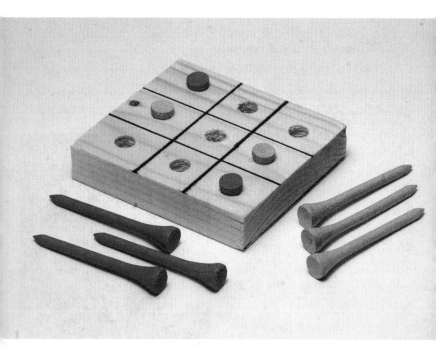

3. Determine the type of wood needed. If your instructions do not tell you the type of wood you need for your project, you can decide this by asking yourself some questions.

* Do I want to paint or stain my project? Some woods might hold paint better than stain. Also, you may want to paint an inexpensive wood that has some flaws. But you may choose to stain one that has lots of color or pattern.

* Does my project need sturdy wood to hold it up (like a stool, chair, or a table)? Using the wrong wood type might mean you end up sitting on the floor!

* Is my project a showpiece (like a stand for a pinewood derby car) that will show off a pretty color or pattern of wood? Using wood with a pretty color or an interesting pattern is a fun way to make the project more attractive.

* Will my project ever be outside? If your project will stay outside (like a flower box), use a strong wood that takes paint well. Also use a good sealant so the weather won't damage it.

By answering these questions, you will determine the right type of wood for your project.

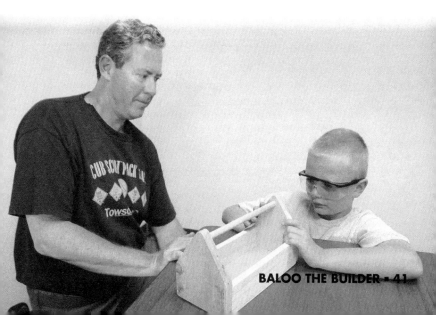

Here are common types of wood:

- Pine, cedar, fir, cypress, and spruce are soft and easy to work with.
- Oak, walnut, hickory, maple, birch, and elm are hard and more sturdy.
- Oak and walnut have interesting grains.
- Cedar has pretty colors and a nice smell.

Since different types of trees grow in different parts of the country, is there another type of wood where you live that is good for projects?

If the type of wood you want to use is not important, think about finding wood that has been recycled. Your parent or den leader can help you locate a place to find recycled wood. Some ideas are house construction sites, cabinet shops, or wooden pallet companies.

2 _____   _____
       Date   **Den Leader's OK**

Useful projects include things like toolboxes. Fun projects include things like tic-tac-toe boards. With your parent or den leader, pick one useful and one fun project, and build both.

Below are some ideas to get you started. You may also choose projects that aren't listed here. Your local or school library is a good place to begin searching for projects.

TOOLBOX OR ART CADDY

Materials and Tools

- Five 1- by 6-inch pieces of wood to be cut to various lengths
- Broomstick piece or dowel, 18 inches long, for the handle
- Wood screws
- Wood glue
- Hand saw
- Brace and bit
- Screwdriver
- Measuring tape

Instructions

1. Cut two pieces of wood 17½ inches long for the two long sides.

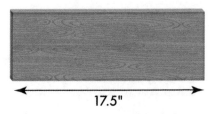

17.5"

2. Cut one piece of wood 16 inches long for the bottom.

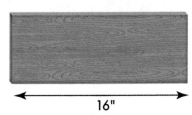

16"

3. Cut two pieces of wood 10 inches long for the ends.

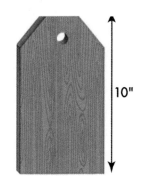

10"

4. Cut off the corners of the end pieces at an angle, then drill a hole in each large enough for the handle. The center of each hole should be 1¾ inch from the top and centered between the edges of the piece.

5. Insert the handle. Then, put your toolbox together with wood screws. If you wish, you may put wood glue on the joints and let it dry before using the wood screws.

6. Finish your toolbox using one of the methods described in requirement 4.

BOOKENDS

Cut these easy bookends from one piece of wood.

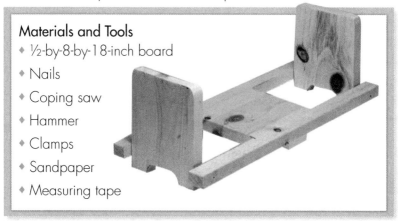

Materials and Tools

◆ ½-by-8-by-18-inch board
◆ Nails
◆ Coping saw
◆ Hammer
◆ Clamps
◆ Sandpaper
◆ Measuring tape

Instructions

1. Cut a 1-inch wide piece from the end of the board and set aside. You will use this piece later as a support for the middle.

2. At each end of the board, measure and draw the pieces to be cut out for the ends. Measure approximately one-third the distance from each end toward the center of the board. This will be the line to cut across the board. Measure 1½ inch from the long edge of the board toward the center on each side. These will be your long cuts on the board.

3. Carefully cut out each of the pieces.

4. Nail the cutout pieces in an upright position at the ends of the remaining piece of board according to the illustration so that the board is 1 inch off the table.

5. Nail the 1-inch piece that you cut off at the beginning under the middle of the board to provide support. Use a short nail for this step.

6. Sand and finish as desired.

SAILING SHIP

Materials and Tools
* Two pieces of 1-by-4-inch board
* Heavy cardstock
* Three 10-inch-long pieces of ⅛-inch dowel
* Wood glue
* Saw
* Small hole punch
* Scissors
* Sandpaper
* Brace and bit

Instructions
1. Cut each piece of board as shown in the illustration.
2. Sand all edges smooth.
3. Drill three holes into the pieces of the ship about halfway through the wood as shown: one into the center of the base, one into the prow block, and one into the stern block to accommodate dowels for the masts. (The holes should be large enough so the one-eighth inch dowels fit into them.)
4. Stack the pieces as shown and glue.
5. Dip one end of each dowel in glue, and insert into the drilled holes for masts.
6. Cut three sails from heavy cardstock, and color as desired. Punch holes where indicated, and slide onto each mast.

_____   _____
Date   **Den Leader's OK**

REQUIREMENT 4 | Apply a finish to one of your projects.

Once you have completed your project, you may want to put a finish on it. There are many ways to finish the wood. How you are going to use your project will help guide you in selecting the correct method of finishing it. Ask a parent or guardian to help with handling the finishes and cleaning fluids.

Always sand projects before you finish them. Sand the wood with the grain, never against it or in circles. To get the best results from sanding, use a wood filler for scratches and holes. When the filler dries, sand the project lightly again.

You can use several finishes on wood projects: acrylics, varnish, enamel, and wood stains. Apply a clear wax polish to raw wood to emphasize the beauty of the natural wood grain.

Here are some things you should know about different finishes.

♦ Acrylics: Acrylic paint is nontoxic and good for painting almost anything, including wood projects. It can be thinned with water and doesn't need a finishing coat. Clean your brushes with water.

♦ Varnish: Prepare wood with one or two coats of thin shellac or wood sealer first, sanding between coats. This will fill the pores of the wood and prepare it for varnishing. Use shellac thinner or alcohol to clean the shellac brush, turpentine to clean the varnish brush.

◆ Enamel paint: Prepare wood in the same manner as for varnishing. Two thin coats of enamel produce a colorful finish. If it is too thick, it will leave brush strokes. Clean the brush with turpentine.

◆ Wood stain: To prepare the wood, moisten it with turpentine before applying the stain. Experiment on a scrap of wood to make sure the results please you. If it is too thick, it will leave brush strokes. Clean the brush with turpentine.

Remember to get help from your parent or den leader before you begin this part of your project. Always use finishes in a well-ventilated area. It is a good idea to wear a simple paint mask and eye protection as well.

4

Date

Den Leader's OK

BEAR CLAWS

REQUIRED ADVENTURE

Complete the following requirements.

1. Learn about three common designs of pocketknives.

2. Learn knife safety and earn your Whittling Chip. *

3. Do one of the following:

   A. Using a pocketknife, carve two items.

   B. With a pocketknife, safely perform each of these tasks:

   (1) Demonstrate how to cut a piece of rope, twine, or fishing line.

   (2) Open a sealed box without damaging the contents.

   (3) Open a can with the can opener tool on a pocketknife.

   (4) Remove and replace the screws on an object with the screwdriver tool on a pocketknife.

   (5) Open a letter.

Pocketknives are great tools to have on campouts. You can use them to carve hiking sticks, cut up food when you are cooking, and even open bottles and cans. But you have to know how to use them the right way in order to stay safe. Learning to use pocketknives—and making neat things with them—is what this adventure is all about.

*One of the items carved for Bear Claws requirement 3 may be used to fulfill Whittling Chip requirement 3.

SNAPSHOT OF ADVENTURE

A pocketknife is a useful tool to have for Scouting activities. It can also be dangerous if you don't use it the right way. In this adventure, you will learn how to use a pocketknife safely. You will also get to learn the basics of carving.

A Scout is trustworthy. You can show that you are trustworthy by taking care of your pocketknife and using it safely.

**COMPLETE REQUIREMENTS 1 AND 2 AND
EITHER 3A OR 3B FOR THIS ADVENTURE.**

REQUIREMENT 1 | Learn about three common designs of pocketknives.

Pocketknives come in all shapes and sizes. Some can be used for many different tasks. Others are designed for special purposes like fishing.

Three common designs used in Scouting are the jackknife, the penknife, and the multipurpose knife. Let's look at each type.

JACKKNIFE

A jackknife is a good tool for campers and fishermen. It is hinged at only one end and may have one or two blades. Sometimes one blade has a very sharp point, while another blade has a more rounded point.

Some jackknives (and other knives) have locking blades. That means you have to push a release before you can close the blade. Locking blades prevent you from accidentally closing the blade on your fingers.

PENKNIFE

A penknife is small and lightweight, so it is easy to carry in your pocket. It is hinged at both ends and usually has one or two blades at each end. Penknives were originally designed to cut or sharpen quills used for writing. Thomas Jefferson wrote the Declaration of Independence with a quill pen.

MULTIPURPOSE KNIFE

Multipurpose knives can be used to do many things. In addition to one or two blades, a multipurpose knife might include a can opener, scissors, leather punch, tweezers, and screwdrivers.

These knives can be fun to have, but all those extra pieces can get in your way when you are just trying to carve or cut some string. Also, the more tools your knife includes, the heavier it will be. Pick a multipurpose knife that has only the tools you really need.

1

Date   **Den Leader's OK**

REQUIREMENT 2 | Learn knife safety and earn your Whittling Chip.*

It is very important to be safe when you use your pocketknife. In this requirement, you will learn the rules of knife safety and earn your Whittling Chip. When you have earned your Whittling Chip, you will be allowed to carry your pocketknife to designated Cub Scout activities. Your parent or den leader will tell you when you may bring your knife. Always keep your Whittling Chip card with you when you are carrying your knife.

 A Scout is obedient. When you follow the rules of knife safety, you keep yourself from getting hurt and you show that you are obedient.

KNIFE SAFETY RULES TO LEARN AND LIVE BY

* A knife is a tool, not a toy.

* Know how to sharpen a knife. A sharp knife is safer than a dull knife because it is less likely to slip and cut you.

* Keep the blade clean and dry.

* Never carry an open pocketknife.

* When you are not using your knife, close it using the palm of your hand and put it away.

* When you are using the cutting blade, do not try to make big shavings or chips. Cut slowly and steadily.

* Make a safety circle. Before you pick up your knife to use it, stretch your arm out and turn in a circle. If you cannot touch anyone or anything else, it is safe to use your knife. While using your knife, be sure to watch in case someone walks toward you and gets too close. If that happens, put your knife away until it is safe to continue.

*One of the items carved for Bear Claws requirement 3 may be used to fulfill Whittling Chip requirement 3.

- Always cut away from you, never toward you.
- Never hand a knife to someone else blade first. Learn and use the "eye contact" method of handing a knife to someone else. Do not release the knife until the other person makes eye contact with you and acknowledges he or she is receiving the knife.
- Never use a knife on something that will dull or break it.
- Never throw a knife for any reason.
- Always think before you cut. Do not use your knife to strip bark from a tree or to carve your initials into something that does not belong to you.

Once you understand the safety rules, agree to abide by the Pocketknife Pledge, complete your project, and have your den leader sign your card, you will have earned your Whittling Chip.

POCKETKNIFE PLEDGE

I understand the reason for safety rules.

I will treat my pocketknife with the respect due a useful tool.

I will always close my pocketknife and put it away when I am not using it.

I will not use my pocketknife when it might injure someone near me.

I promise never to throw my pocketknife for any reason.

I will use my pocketknife in a safe manner at all times.

KEEPING YOUR KNIFE SHARP

A good way to sharpen your knife is to use a sharpening stone. Lay the blade on the stone at a slight angle. Push the blade forward as if you were going to shave a thin sliver from the stone. Do not push down hard. Next, turn the blade over and shave the stone toward you. This is the only time you should move your knife toward yourself. Keep your fingers below the surface of the stone to protect them. Continue this back-and-forth action until the edge is sharp along its entire length.

MAKING STOP CUTS

Here is a secret to use when you are whittling. Before you make a shaving cut, make a stop cut. At the place you want the shaving to stop, cut straight down with your knife. Press down and rock the blade back and forth until the cut is as deep as you want the shaving to go. This stop cut will prevent you from shaving off too much wood.

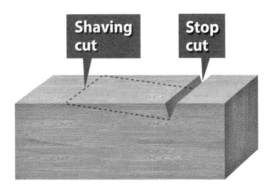

Shaving cut

Stop cut

FIRST AID FOR KNIFE CUTS

Accidents can happen even when you are being careful. It is important that you know what to do if you or one of your fellow Scouts gets cut while using a pocketknife.

Small cuts in the skin can allow bacteria to enter the body and cause infection. Wash minor cuts with soap and water. Apply antibiotic ointment and cover with a dry, sterile dressing or an adhesive bandage to help prevent infection and protect the wound. Clean and rebandage wounds each day. If the cut is more serious, get help from an adult immediately.

Taking proper care of a wound will help prevent other health issues like an infection.

2

_____   _____
Date   Den Leader's OK

COMPLETE REQUIREMENT 3A OR 3B.

REQUIREMENT 3A | Using a pocketknife, carve two items.

It is fun to whittle sticks, but it is even more fun to make carvings of things like animals, acorns, and space aliens. A good way to learn to carve is to practice with a bar of soap. Carve a simple item and then try something a little harder.

What You Will Need

♦ A large bar of soap—it is best to unwrap the soap and let it dry for a day or two before you start carving

♦ A pocketknife

♦ One or two orangewood sticks (used for manicures) or a sheet of tracing paper

♦ Paper for sketching a design or a preprinted pattern

♦ A tray to work on—this will keep chips and shavings from going everywhere

WHAT TO DO

1. Choose a simple design that does not have too many projections or fine details. Start simple. You can pick a fancier design for your next carving.

2. Prepare the soap. Cut away the raised edges on the soap and scrape off the lettering. This will give you a nice, smooth block to work with.

3. Sketch the outline of your design on the soap. You can do this by drawing with an orangewood stick or by tracing your design using tracing paper.

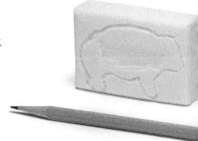

4. Make your first rough cuts. Cut away small pieces and slices of the soap that are not part of your design. Do not cut big pieces; if you do, the soap might break. Leave a margin of about one-quarter inch outside your outline.

5. Shape the model. Continue carving so you get closer and closer to your outline. Keep turning the soap to work on all parts of your design. Do not try to finish one part before another. Pay special attention to high points and low points on the carving.

6. Polish your carving. Let the soap dry for a day or two, then rub it gently to smooth it out. Use a paper napkin first and then your fingertips.

7. Add detail. Finally, use your knife to add details like eyes or hair. If you like, create a crisscross pattern to give the carving more depth.

3A _____   _____

        Date   **Den Leader's OK**

REQUIREMENT 3B | With a pocketknife, safely perform each of these tasks:

1. Demonstrate how to cut a piece of rope, twine, or fishing line.
2. Open a sealed box without damaging the contents.
3. Open a can with the can opener tool on a pocketknife.
4. Remove and replace the screws on an object with the screwdriver tool on a pocketknife.
5. Open a letter.

3B _____   _____

        Date   **Den Leader's OK**

BEAR NECESSITIES

REQUIRED ADVENTURE

Complete requirements 1–4. Requirements 5 and 6 are optional.

1. While working on your Bear badge, attend one of the following:

   A. A daytime or overnight campout with your pack or family

   B. An outdoor activity with your den or pack

   C. Day camp

   D. Resident camp

2. Make a list of items you should take along on the activity selected in requirement 1.

3. Make a list of equipment that the group should bring along in addition to each Scout's personal gear for the activity selected in requirement 1.

4. Help set up a tent. Determine a good spot for the tent, and explain to your den leader why you picked it.

5. Demonstrate how to tie two half hitches and explain what the hitch is used for.

6. Learn how to read a thermometer and a barometer. Keep track of the temperature and barometric pressure readings and the actual weather at the same time every day for seven days.

SNAPSHOT OF ADVENTURE

A bear is at home in the outdoors, and so is a Bear Scout! In this adventure, you'll learn how to plan and set up a campsite, cook a meal with your den, and watch for changes in the weather. But best of all, you'll get to go camping! Are you ready?

REQUIREMENT 1 | While working on your Bear badge, attend one of the following:

Scouts love camping because they know how to take care of themselves outdoors. For this requirement, go on a camping adventure. This could be a pack overnighter, an outdoor activity with your den or pack, or attendance at a day camp or resident camp.

REQUIREMENT 1A | A daytime or overnight campout with your pack or family

REQUIREMENT 1B | An outdoor activity with your den or pack

REQUIREMENT 1C | Day camp

REQUIREMENT 1D | Resident camp

_____   _____
Date   Den Leader's OK

Being comfortable in the outdoors means taking along the right gear to keep you warm, dry, and safe. You don't need all the comforts of home, but a few key things can really help you enjoy your campout.

Make a list of personal items you should bring along on your activity, including your Cub Scout Six Essentials. You should take them on every outing. If you need help making your list, your den leader may have some ideas to help out.

CUB SCOUT SIX ESSENTIALS

First-aid kit	Flashlight	Sun protection
Filled water bottle	Trail food	Whistle

On our activity I'll need:

_____

_____

_____

_____

_____

_____

Be sure to bring this gear along.

2

_____   _____
Date   Den Leader's OK

REQUIREMENT 3 | Make a list of equipment that the group should bring along in addition to each Scout's personal gear for the activity selected in requirement 1.

Besides your personal gear, you will need some other items that the whole group will use. With your den or family, make a list of some of those items below. Your leader will make sure these items are at the campout for the group to use.

Our group will need:

_____

_____

_____

_____

_____

_____

_____

_____

3

_____   _____
        Date   Den Leader's OK

Where you put up your tent is an important part of being comfortable on a campout. Your tent should be in a flat area that is clear of any low spots where water will collect if it rains. It should also be sheltered from strong winds. During cold weather, try to face the door of your tent away from the wind.

Before you put up your tent, move any rocks, sticks, or other hard objects from the tent site. They can hurt bare feet and damage the bottom of your tent.

After you take down the tent, put back the objects you moved near where you found them. Also, pick up anything you and other campers brought to the campsite. Scouts always leave no trace!

4

Date   Den Leader's OK

Every knot has a specific use. The two half hitches knot is used to tie items to a post or tree trunk. The knot is easy to untie when you are ready, but it will hold tight while in use. Each wrap around the rope is called a half hitch. Making two of them around the rope is what gives this hitch its name.

Tie a rope to a tree or post using two half hitches, then pull hard. Did the knot hold? Now stop pulling, and see how easy it is to untie. Just push the free end of the rope back through, and the knot is untied!

Date   Den Leader's OK

Have you ever watched weather forecasters on TV and wondered how they know what the weather will be tomorrow? They use many tools to report and predict the weather.

One important tool is a thermometer, which tells how hot or cold it is. What is the hottest weather you've ever felt? What is the coldest?

Another important tool is a barometer. It reads barometric pressure, which is the pressure the air in the atmosphere places on the ground. Keeping track of changes in barometric pressure can tell us how the weather will change. If the pressure is falling, a storm is probably coming. If the pressure is steady or rising gently, the weather should be calm and nice!

A Scout is cheerful. It's easy to be cheerful when the weather on a campout is great. If you are prepared with the right gear, you can also be cheerful on a rainy day.

Pay attention to how the weather feels to you when you know the temperature. You'll be able to better prepare for outings that way. When the temperature is going to be 50 degrees during the day, you know you'll need a jacket!

Understanding barometric pressure and weather forecasts can also help you be better prepared for outings. If you know that afternoon storms are likely, you can change your campout schedule to hike in the morning and stay close to camp in the afternoon.

Use this chart to track the weather for a week. Take temperature and pressure readings at the same time every day so you can compare. Circle whether the pressure is rising or falling for each day. In the last column, write a description like "sunny and breezy" or "heavy rain."

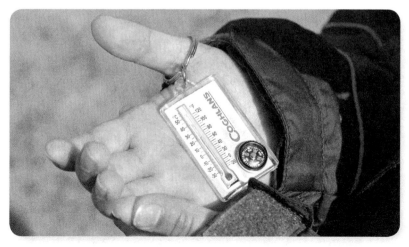

You can get your readings using a thermometer and a barometer. Or, with your parent's or guardian's help, you can also find temperature and pressure readings on the internet or your local television news broadcast.

WEATHER-TRACKING CHART

Date	Temperature	Barometric Pressure	Change	Weather
1.	_____degrees	_____inches/mm	rising/falling	
2.	_____degrees	_____inches/mm	rising/falling	
3.	_____degrees	_____inches/mm	rising/falling	
4.	_____degrees	_____inches/mm	rising/falling	
5.	_____degrees	_____inches/mm	rising/falling	
6.	_____degrees	_____inches/mm	rising/falling	
7.	_____degrees	_____inches/mm	rising/falling	

6

_____
Date

_____
Den Leader's OK

FELLOWSHIP AND DUTY TO GOD

REQUIRED ADVENTURE

Complete the following requirements.

1. Discuss with your parent, guardian, den leader, or other caring adult what it means to do your duty to God. Tell how you do your duty to God in your daily life.

2. Complete at least one of the following:

   A. Identify a person whose faith you admire, and discuss this person with your family.

   B. With a family member, provide service to a place of worship or a spiritual community, school, or community organization that puts into practice your ideals of duty to God and strengthens your fellowship with others.

3. Complete at least one of the following:

   A. Earn the religious emblem of your faith that is appropriate for your age, if you have not already done so.

   B. Make a list of things you can do to practice your duty to God as you are taught in your home or place of worship or spiritual community. Select two of the items and practice them for two weeks.

SNAPSHOT OF ADVENTURE

Just about every religion teaches the Golden Rule: "Treat others the way you would want to be treated." The Golden Rule is a good rule to follow every day, and it's one way we can practice our duty to God. Practicing the Golden Rule is a big part of this adventure. When we treat family members with kindness, help our neighbors, and reach out to people in our community, we help make life better for everyone. We become happier, and our faith in God is strengthened. In this adventure, you will get to practice your duty to God by helping people around you.

Maybe that's what Robert Baden-Powell, who invented Scouting, meant when he said every Scout should do a Good Turn every day.

Note to Parents and Other Caring Adults

Inspiration and support for your child's spiritual development will come primarily from your family and/or faith leaders. While reverence and duty to God have always been part of Boy Scout values, the Boy Scouts of America does not promote any specific religion and is completely nonsectarian. There is no requirement that Scouts identify with a particular religion or faith.

In keeping with these principles, your Scout will need your guidance to complete requirements for the Fellowship and Duty to God adventure. Please let the den leader know when your Scout has completed each requirement.

COMPLETE THE FOLLOWING REQUIREMENTS.

REQUIREMENT 1 | Discuss with your parent, guardian, den leader, or other caring adult what it means to do your duty to God. Tell how you do your duty to God in your daily life.

Think about the Golden Rule idea of treating others the way you'd like to be treated. What are some examples of things you do every day that show that you use the Golden Rule? How are you kind to other people? What do you do to help other people? Are there things that you do that make life better for someone else?

Think about the last point of the Scout Law: A Scout is reverent. Dictionaries tell us that being reverent means being respectful. What do you do in your daily life to show respect? Remember that Scouts respect nature as well as other people. How do your daily actions show that you respect the world around you?

Date   Den Leader's OK

Note to Parents and Other Caring Adults

Please let your Scout's den leader know when this requirement has been completed.

REQUIREMENT 2A | Identify a person whose faith you admire, and discuss this person with your family.

Many people throughout history have shown great faith in God by reaching out to people in their neighborhoods and communities. They freely gave their time and talent to help other people.

Here are some individuals who helped other people because of their faith. Find out more about one of these individuals or another person with a strong background of faith. What can you learn from what that person did?

Roger Williams started the colony of Rhode Island so he and his friends could practice their faith freely. He was a friend to American Indians and worked to prohibit slavery in the colonies.

Job Ben Solomon was a Muslim leader from Africa who was enslaved in the colony of Georgia. His intelligence and faithfulness may have helped convince the colony's founder, James Oglethorpe, to turn against slavery.

Barbara Heck was an Irish immigrant who helped found the first Methodist church in New York. At a time when women didn't tell men what to do, she convinced Philip Embury to lead the new church.

Father Pierre-Jean De Smet was known as Black Robe by Native Americans. He was a Catholic missionary in the American West and made friends with American Indians and with pioneers of different religions.

Abraham Lincoln did not go to any particular church, but he had a strong belief in God.

That belief led him to decide that all people should be free and helped him win the Civil War, which freed the slaves.

Brigham Young was a pioneer leader of the Church of Jesus Christ of Latter-day Saints, which is also known as the Mormon church. He helped establish many settlements in the western United States where Mormons could practice their religion in peace.

Jacob Schiff was a German-born American businessman. He worked hard to help Jewish people come to America between 1880 and 1920 and feel welcome here.

Jane Addams was inspired by her religious faith to improve the lives of children and immigrants. She helped turn a rundown Chicago mansion into a settlement house where people could get assistance and learn what it means to be an American.

Daisho Tana was a Buddhist priest who ministered to fellow Japanese Americans who were removed from their homes during World War II. He helped them practice their religion in difficult circumstances.

The Reverend Martin Luther King Jr. relied on his Christian faith in his nonviolent struggles for equal rights in America. He showed that by loving your enemies you can sometimes turn them into friends.

Cesar Chavez relied on his Catholic traditions in his work to help Hispanics and migrant farm workers earn civil rights and respect. He also used principles of nonviolent protest and developed the slogan, "¡Sí, se puede!" ("Yes! It can be done!").

Who I researched: _____

_____

Characteristics I liked about this person: _____

_____

_____

What I learned from this experience: _____

_____

_____

_____

_____

Date   **Den Leader's OK**

A Scout is reverent. Part of being reverent is living by your family's faith traditions.

REQUIREMENT 2B | **With a family member, provide service to a place of worship or a spiritual community, school, or community organization that puts into practice your ideals of duty to God and strengthens your fellowship with others.**

Cub Scouts are good at helping people. So are people of faith. When you serve others, you also serve and honor God.

There are lots of ways to help people and do your duty to God. You can collect food, clothes, or toys for people who are less fortunate. You can read and play games with children. You can rake leaves for elderly people in your community or visit people who live in a senior living center.

Think about people you might help and then talk with your parent or another trusted adult about ways you could help them. After your service project, write down what you did and how you felt about your experience.

MY SERVICE PROJECT

The people I served: _____

_____

What I did: _____

_____

_____

The people who worked with me: _____

_____

_____

_____

How helping other people made me feel: _____

_____

_____

_____

A Scout is helpful. You can show you are helpful by participating in service projects.

2B

Date   Den Leader's OK

Note to Parents and Other Caring Adults

Please let your Scout's den leader know when this requirement has been completed.

REQUIREMENT 3A | Earn the religious emblem of your faith that is appropriate for your age, if you have not already done so.

A religious emblem is a special award that you can earn for learning about God.

Many major faith groups have emblems that Scouts can earn. Your pack or den leaders can help you and your family find more information about the religious emblems for your faith.

3A

_____   _____
Date   Den Leader's OK

Note to Parents and Other Caring Adults

Please let your Scout's den leader know when this requirement has been completed.

Every faith tradition has things its members are supposed to do. Some of those things draw you closer to God, like praying and going to worship services. Some of those things draw you closer to other people, like serving and offering help to others in need.

Make a list of things you can do to practice your duty to God.

Your list might include praying each day, reading inspirational poems or books of faith, singing hymns, doing chores with a positive attitude, helping classmates with their homework, or using good manners.

_____

_____

_____

_____

Circle two practices from your list that you will do for two weeks. At the end of the two weeks, explain what you did.

3B

_____ _____
Date   **Den Leader's OK**

Note to Parents and Other Caring Adults

Please let your Scout's den leader know when this requirement has been completed.

FUR, FEATHERS, AND FERNS

REQUIRED ADVENTURE

Complete requirement 1 plus three others.

1. While hiking or walking for one mile, identify six signs that any mammals, birds, insects, reptiles, or plants are living near the place where you choose to hike or walk.

2. Visit one of the following: zoo, wildlife refuge, nature center, aviary, game preserve, local conservation area, wildlife rescue group, or fish hatchery. Describe what you learned during your visit.

3. Name one animal that has become extinct in the last 100 years and one animal that is currently endangered. Explain what caused their declines.

4. Observe wildlife from a distance. Describe what you saw.

5. Use a magnifying glass to examine plants more closely. Describe what you saw through the magnifying glass that you could not see without it.

6. Learn about composting and how vegetable waste can be turned into fertilizer for plants.

7. Plant a vegetable or herb garden.

SNAPSHOT OF ADVENTURE

In this adventure you will explore the world of mammals, birds, plants, and more. You will learn more about where wild creatures live and you will do your part to help them. You will practice the Outdoor Code by showing ways to be considerate in the outdoors. So grab your binoculars and start exploring the natural world.

A Scout is kind. You can show you are kind to animals by protecting their habitat.

COMPLETE REQUIREMENT 1 PLUS THREE OTHERS.

REQUIREMENT 1 | While hiking or walking for one mile, identify six signs that any mammals, birds, insects, reptiles, or plants are living near the place where you choose to hike or walk.

Do you remember that as a Cub Scout you must always Do Your Best? One way is to prepare for hiking by warming up your muscles.

To warm up for your hike, walk or jog for a few minutes and then do these stretches. When you stretch, don't bounce. Just move gently until you feel your muscles start to stretch.

Quadriceps (muscles in the front of your thighs): Stand up and hold on to a sturdy support. Grab your left ankle and bring it up behind you. With your knees close together, push your hips forward until you feel the muscles stretching. Hold for 20 seconds. Repeat on the other side.

FUR, FEATHERS, AND FERNS ▪ 89

Abductors (muscles in your hips, bottom, and sides of your thighs): Sit on the floor with your right leg straight out. Bend your left leg so your left foot is to the right of your right knee. Twist your upper body to the left until you feel the muscles stretching. Hold for 20 seconds. Repeat on the other side.

Hamstrings (muscles on the backs of your thighs): Sit on the floor with your right leg straight out and your left leg bent. With your back straight, bend forward from your hips, reaching toward your right foot. Hold for 20 seconds. Repeat on the other side.

Hip Flexors (muscles in your hips that flex your thigh bones): Kneel on the floor, then position your right leg so your right foot is in front of you and your right knee forms a 90 degree angle. Push forward with your hips, keeping them as square as possible. Hold for 20 seconds. Repeat on the other side.

Calves (muscles in your lower legs): Stand up and take a big step forward with your right leg. Keep your left leg straight. Lean forward a little so that your body and left leg form a straight line. Hold for 20 seconds. Repeat on the other side.

Take a 1-mile hike with your den or a family member. Bring binoculars and a notebook and pencil to take notes or a camera or smartphone to take pictures. Be sure to pack your Cub Scout Six Essentials.

CUB SCOUT SIX ESSENTIALS

First-aid kit

Flashlight
(check the batteries)

Sun protection

Filled water bottle

Trail food

Whistle

As you walk, look up, down, and all around for signs that mammals, reptiles, insects, or birds have been there. Also look for different types of plants. Write down what you see.

Here are some things to look for:

◆ Partly chewed leaves or flowers that insects or mammals have left

◆ Slime trails that show where snails have traveled

◆ A bird flying by with a leaf or twig in its beak on its way to build a nest nearby

◆ Scratch marks on a tree where an animal has marked its territory

◆ Holes that lead to the underground home of a mammal, reptile, or insect

◆ Animal scat (droppings) that indicates a creature ate a meal nearby

HIKE LOG

Animal Signs I Saw	Actual Animals I Saw	Plants I Saw
_____	_____	_____
_____	_____	_____
_____	_____	_____
_____	_____	_____
_____	_____	_____
_____	_____	_____

All Scouts learn and follow the Outdoor Code. As Bears, you'll focus on the part of the Outdoor Code that says to be considerate in the outdoors. Two of the Leave No Trace Principles for Kids go right along with that idea. Those principles are "Leave What You Find" and "Be Kind to Other Visitors."

After your hike, discuss with your den leader ways that you demonstrated those principles. How do those principles support the Outdoor Code?

1

Date   **Den Leader's OK**

Many organizations and government agencies work to protect animals and plants. Some of them have facilities you can visit to learn more about their work and perhaps see the creatures they protect.

You may even be able to help them help those creatures! Agencies like the U.S. Fish and Wildlife Service use volunteers to remove invasive species, conduct wildlife surveys, plant native grasses along riverbanks, and put identification bands on migratory birds.

2 _____   _____
        Date   **Den Leader's OK**

An animal species becomes extinct when its last member dies. Extinction happens for many reasons, including loss of habitat, overhunting, climate change, or the appearance of a new predator or disease.

You've heard of animals like dinosaurs that became extinct millions of years ago. But some animals became extinct more recently. A good example is the passenger pigeon. When Europeans first came to North America, there were billions of passenger pigeons. In the 1700s, a man named Cotton Mather wrote about a flock of birds that was a mile wide and took several hours to pass overhead!

Passenger pigeons were an important source of food in the 1800s, and they were hunted nearly to extinction. A few survived in captive flocks, but the last passenger pigeon, Martha (named after Martha Washington), died in 1914 at the Cincinnati Zoo.

Not all stories have sad endings. After World War II, the American bald eagle was in serious decline. A pesticide called DDT was poisoning the fish that eagles liked to eat and hurting the eagles. In 1967, the species was listed as endangered.

DDT was banned in the United States in 1972, which helped eagles rebound. Conservationists also worked hard to breed captive eagles, reintroduce them into nature, and protect their nest sites. By 1995, bald eagles were listed as threatened, which is better than endangered. In 2007, the species was removed from the list of threatened and endangered species altogether. (It is still illegal to kill, sell, or possess bald eagles without special permission.)

THREATENED, ENDANGERED, AND EXTINCT

"Threatened" means a species is likely to become endangered if people don't work to protect it.

"Endangered" means a species is likely to become extinct in all or a major part of its natural habitat.

"Extinct" means a species no longer exists.

Extinct animal: _____

Endangered animal: _____

 You can learn about threatened and endangered species in your area by visiting **www.fws.gov/endangered** with your parent's or guardian's permission.

There are many reasons to conserve threatened and endangered species, whether plants or animals:

- Contributions to medicine. Many important medicines come from plants. For example, scientists make cancer medicine from the bark of the Pacific yew tree.

- Contributions to agriculture. Birds and insects pollinate one third of the food we eat. For example, bees pollinate fruit and nut trees and melon vines.

- Environmental monitors. Problems with animal species can alert humans to dangers to our planet. For example, the decline in bald eagles helped people discover that DDT was dangerous.

* Keeping the food chain going. Animals and plants are part of a food chain that provides food for other animals (including us!). For example, eagles eat snakes, which eat mice, which eat crickets. If crickets became extinct, mice, snakes, and eagles could all go hungry.

* Beauty. Nothing compares with the beauty of nature!

"Keep close to Nature's heart ... and break clear away, once in a while, and climb a mountain or spend a week in the woods. Wash your spirit clean." – *John Muir, naturalist and co-founder of the Sierra Club*

3

Date   Den Leader's OK

If you've ever seen an animal in the wild, you know how exciting watching wildlife can be. It is important to watch from a distance, however. Some animals can be dangerous to you. Also, you don't want to scare an animal off or disturb it while it is eating.

A good place to spot wildlife is along shorelines. Even if you don't see any animals, you'll probably find lots of footprints where they've come down to get a drink.

Some wildlife refuges and parks have blinds that you can get behind to watch birds and other animals. A blind is a camouflaged wall or shelter with windows in it. Sometimes, one-way glass is used so that you can see the animals but the animals can't see you.

You can also use a periscope to peek over a wall or around a corner at wildlife. The directions below show how to make a simple periscope out of milk cartons. A field guide will help you identify what you see.

 Check with your den leader or another adult before using a knife or scissors for this activity.

MAKE A CARDBOARD PERISCOPE

1. Cut the tops off two quart-sized milk (or similar style) cartons.

2. Cut a square hole on one side of one carton, just above the bottom. Leave a ¼-inch border around the hole.

3. On the sides to the left and right of the hole, cut slits at a 45-degree angle. The bottom of each slit should be near the edge close to the hole. The top of each slit should be near the edge away from the hole.

4. Slide a mirror into the slot with the reflecting side facing the hole. Tape it in place so it doesn't fall out.

5. Repeat steps 2 through 4 with the other milk carton.

6. Slightly crimp the open end of one milk carton. Slide that carton into the open end of the other one with the holes facing in opposite directions. Tape the two cartons together.

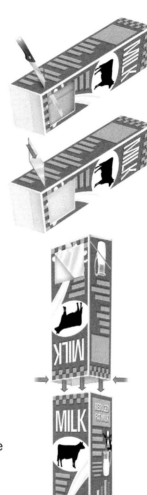

4

_____   _____
Date   **Den Leader's OK**

Plants are beautiful at a distance, but sometimes they are even more fun to look at up close. When you examine a plant with a magnifying glass, you can see all sorts of things that are hidden from the naked eye.

What can you see? You can see the veins that form a leaf's skeleton. You can see tiny aphids sucking sap out of a plant stem. You can see drops of dew rolling down pine needles. You can see the tiny seeds that make up the eye of a sunflower.

Grab a magnifying glass and start looking!

The Outdoor Code (found in the back of your book) reminds Scouts to be considerate in the outdoors. One of the ways you can show consideration is by following the Leave No Trace principle of "Leave What You Find." Let future hikers enjoy the plants you see as well. Instead of taking souvenirs, use the space below to jot notes or draw a picture of your observations.

Date

Den Leader's OK

REQUIREMENT 6 | Learn about composting and how vegetable waste can be turned into fertilizer for plants.

When you eat a banana, do you throw the peel away? When you scrape extra food off your plate at dinner, where does it go? You can actually turn banana peels, food scraps, grass clippings, and even paper into fertilizer for plants by composting.

Composting is a process where you mix organic materials in a pile or a container, along with a little water. Worms and insects chew up the material and help good bacteria grow in it. In a month or two, you end up with a dark, rich fertilizer that you can spread around plants to help them grow.

You can make a compost pile in the corner of your yard, or you can use a special composting container. As you learn about composting, find out about any regulations your local community may have. This page shows how to make a compost bin out of an old trash can.

BUILD A COMPOST BIN

Find a plastic trash can with a tight-fitting lid.

Ask an adult to drill or punch 10 air holes around the can near the top edge.

Ask an adult to drill or punch 20 drain holes in the bottom, each one-quarter inch or three-eighths of an inch in diameter.

Dig a hole about 15 inches deep in a corner of your yard that drains well.

Set the can in the hole and push the dirt from the hole up around it.

Start composting!

Here are some things that can go into your compost pile or container:

- Table scraps (nothing greasy or containing meat)
- Fruit and vegetable scraps
- Crushed eggshells
- Leaves
- Grass clippings (in thin layers)
- Pine needles (in moderate amounts)
- Flowers and chopped stems
- Coffee grounds and filters
- Tea leaves and tea bags
- Newspaper and shredded paper (avoid glossy paper and colored ink)
- Shredded cardboard
- Barnyard manure (no dog and cat waste)

Add water from time to time so the compost stays as wet as a damp sponge. Once a week, stir the compost from the outside in. That's all you have to do. The worms and insects will do the rest!

A Scout is thrifty. One way to be thrifty is to keep food out of landfills by composting it.

6

Date   **Den Leader's OK**

REQUIREMENT 7 | Plant a vegetable or herb garden.

Growing your own vegetables and herbs is a fun way to learn how plants grow. And nothing tastes better than food you have grown yourself.

Some people think you have to have a big yard to have a garden, but you can grow vegetables and herbs in a small space using pots or plastic trays.

GROW A PIZZA GARDEN

If you like pizza, you'll love growing your own herbs to put on it. Fresh herbs make any pizza better, whether you baked it yourself or bought it at a store.

What you need:
- ◆ Some small pots with drainage holes (and trays if your garden will be inside)
- ◆ Potting soil
- ◆ Herb plants like basil, thyme, oregano, rosemary, and parsley
- ◆ A place where the herbs can get lots of sunlight

Thyme   Rosemary   Basil

What to do:

♦ Put some soil in the bottom of each pot so your plants will sit a couple of inches below the top.

♦ Remove the plants from their nursery containers. Place one in each pot and gently fill the pot with soil. Pat the soil down.

♦ Water the plants enough that water runs out the bottom.

♦ Place the pots where they can get sunlight.

♦ Water them when the soil feels dry, and add some fertilizer every two weeks.

♦ Once the herbs grow, just pinch off pieces to put on your pizza. (You can also dry herbs to use later.)

7

_____   _____
Date   Den Leader's OK

PAWS FOR ACTION
(DUTY TO COUNTRY)

REQUIRED ADVENTURE

Complete requirement 1 plus two others from requirements 2–4.

1. Learn about our nation's flag. Display it at home for one month. Say the Pledge of Allegiance, and learn its meaning.

2. Do at least one of the following.

   A. Find out about two famous Americans. Share what you learned.

   B. Find out where places of historical interest are located in or near your community, town, or city. Go and visit one of them with your family or den.

3. Do at least two of the following:

   A. With your school or den, visit a local sheriff's office, police station, or fire department OR talk with a fire safety officer or law enforcement officer visiting your school or den. Find out what skills the officers use to do their jobs. Ask questions that will help you learn how to stay safe.

   B. Make a list of emergency numbers and discuss with your family where the list should be kept. Show your family that you know how to call for help in an emergency. Talk with your family about people who could help you if a parent is not available.

   C. With your family, develop a plan to follow in case of an emergency, and practice the plan at least three times. Your family can determine the emergency, or you can develop several plans.

4. Do at least one of the following:

   A. Do a cleanup project that benefits your community.

   B. Participate in a patriotic community parade or other civic event that honors our country.

SNAPSHOT OF ADVENTURE

This adventure is all about different ways of helping your community and country. You will learn about people who helped make America great and visit a place where history happened. You will learn how law enforcement officers keep your community safe and find out how you can support them. And you will discover ways you can help your community by conserving energy and doing cleanup projects. A Scout is helpful, so let's get started on the Paws for Action adventure!

REQUIREMENT 1 | Learn about our nation's flag. Display it at home for one month. Say the Pledge of Allegiance and learn its meaning.

The United States flag is a very important symbol of our country. We respect the flag because it represents our country and those who have fought to protect it.

The flag was born on June 14, 1777. At first, it had 13 stars and 13 stripes for the 13 original states. As more states joined the United States, it changed many times. Now, the flag has 50 stars, representing

United States flag, 1777

the 50 states, and 13 stripes, representing the original states.

The flag should be treated with courtesy and respect. There are some basic rules every person should know:

- The flag should only be flown from dawn to dusk, unless it is illuminated by a light.

- The flag should only be flown in nice weather, unless it is made of all-weather material.

- You can print out a picture of a flag to display or post a fabric flag outside your home.

- The flag can be displayed every day. Special days to display the flag are holidays like Memorial Day (the last Monday in May), Flag Day (June 14), and Independence Day (July 4).

- The flag should be kept clean, so try not to let it touch the ground. If it does touch the ground, however, it can still be used. If it gets dirty or torn, it's OK to clean and mend it.

- If the flag becomes so dirty, torn, or faded that it can't be used anymore, it should be retired by burning it in a dignified manner. Talk with your den leader or Cubmaster to learn more about retiring ceremonies.

- If you are in uniform, give the Cub Scout salute when the flag passes in a parade, when it is being raised or lowered, or when you are saying the Pledge of Allegiance. If you are not in uniform, hold your right hand over your heart at those times.

One way we show respect to the flag and our country is by reciting the Pledge of Allegiance:

I pledge allegiance to the Flag of the United States of America, and to the Republic for which it stands, one Nation under God, indivisible, with liberty and justice for all.

Talk with your den leader or another adult about what the Pledge of Allegiance means to you. Write it below.

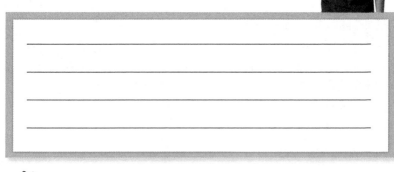

| Date | Den Leader's OK |

DO AT LEAST ONE OF THE FOLLOWING.

REQUIREMENT 2A | Find out about two famous Americans. Share what you learned.

Our country didn't just appear on Earth by magic. Men and women (and children!) worked over hundreds of years to create it. You have learned about some of these people in school.

Here are some famous Americans. Study two of them or other Americans you respect.

Thomas Jefferson was the main author of the Declaration of Independence, which declared that the United States was now independent of Great Britain.

George Washington led the army that won the American Revolution and served as our first president.

William Clark and Meriwether Lewis traveled from St. Louis, Missouri, to the Pacific Ocean to explore the Louisiana Purchase for President Jefferson.

Sequoyah was a Cherokee Indian who created a writing system for the Cherokee language.

Clara Barton created the American Red Cross to help people hurt by wars and natural disasters.

Susan B. Anthony worked tirelessly to help women get the right to vote.

Thomas Edison invented light bulbs, movie cameras, X-ray machines, and much more.

Wilbur and Orville Wright built the first successful airplane.

Rosa Parks helped start the civil rights movement by refusing to give up her seat on a bus in Montgomery, Alabama.

Charles McGee, an Eagle Scout, was a member of the Tuskegee Airmen and flew more than 400 missions during three wars.

Jimmy Carter served as president and later became famous for promoting peace, supporting human rights, and working to end suffering around the world.

Neil Armstrong, an Eagle Scout, was the first human being to stand on the moon.

You can find information about famous Americans in your school or local library, in school textbooks, in social studies class, or on the internet with the help of an adult. Try to find out at least one fact that no one else in your den knows.

Write down what you learn on this page.

MY FAMOUS AMERICANS

Name _____

Birthplace and birthdate _____

How this person helped our country _____

_____

One thing I found out about this person that was very

interesting to me _____

_____

Name _____

Birthplace and birthdate _____

How this person helped our country _____

_____

One thing I found out about this person that was very

interesting to me _____

Share what you learned with your den or family.

There are lots of ways to do this:

- Write a skit for your den to perform.
- Do a solo performance dressed as your character.
- Make a poster showing important things about the person.
- Create a movie on the computer.
- Make a true-false quiz.
- Play a guessing game using facts about the person.

2A _____   _____

REQUIREMENT 2B | Find out where places of historical interest are located in or near your community, town, or city. Go and visit one of them with your family or den.

History is all around us. Learn about and visit a place of historical interest near where you live. This might be the site of an important battle, the place where an exciting discovery happened that is still helping people today, or the home or school of a famous American. Important events might have happened there hundreds of years ago or even since you were born.

A Scout is courteous. You can show courtesy by being on your best behavior when you visit a historic site.

Take along a camera, notebook, or sketchbook to record your visit. Afterward, share what you learned with other people.

MY PLACE OF HISTORICAL INTEREST

The place I visited _____

What makes this place important _____

_____

_____

2B

Date

Den Leader's OK

DO AT LEAST TWO OF THE FOLLOWING:

REQUIREMENT 3A | With your school or den, visit a local sheriff's office, police station, or fire department OR talk with a fire safety officer or law enforcement officer visiting your school or den. Find out what skills the officers use to do their jobs. Ask questions that will help you learn how to stay safe.

Just like a mother bear takes care of her cubs, the adults in your family help keep you safe. There are also people in your community whose job is to keep you and your family safe, even if it means putting their own lives in danger. That's what law enforcement officers do every day to help your community.

Visit with a law enforcement officer at a den meeting or at a local sheriff's office or police station. Learn more about what they do and how you can help keep your family and community safe.

 A Scout is brave. One way to learn about bravery is by asking law enforcement officers how they show bravery in dangerous situations.

Before your visit, think of some questions you could ask. Here are some examples:

- What are some things law enforcement officers do to keep our community safe?
- How do law enforcement officers collect evidence of crimes?
- How realistic are TV shows, movies, and books about crime?
- How can I help prevent crime in my neighborhood?
- How do I get help in an emergency? What phone numbers should I call to get help?
- What should I do if someone I know is being a bully?

3A

_____ _____
Date   Den Leader's OK

REQUIREMENT 3B | Make a list of emergency numbers and discuss with your family where the list should be kept. Show your family that you know how to call for help in an emergency. Talk with your family about people who could help you if a parent is not available.

3B

_____   _____

Date   Den Leader's OK

REQUIREMENT 3C | With your family, develop a plan to follow in case of an emergency and practice the plan at least three times. Your family can determine the emergency, or you can develop several plans.

Emergencies can come in many different forms. Earthquakes, hurricanes, tornadoes, fires, floods, medical emergencies, and lost pets or family members are all examples. To be ready for different types of emergencies, you may need different types of plans and resources. Ask your family members to help you consider what each plan requires. Planning beforehand helps you "BE PREPARED" as all good Scouts should be.

3C

_____   _____

Date   Den Leader's OK

DO AT LEAST ONE OF THE FOLLOWING:

REQUIREMENT 4A | Do a cleanup project that benefits your community.

Cleaning up after ourselves is something we all should do. However, you have probably noticed that not everyone remembers to do that. Sometimes you will see an empty lot where people have dumped trash or where weeds have grown tall. As you travel, you may see trash along the roadside. As a Bear Scout, you can help your community take care of these problems. This is another good way to show pride in your community. By giving your time, you can make a big difference.

With your family or den, discuss a cleanup project you can perform as a group. Plan your project on the next page. Then go do it!

OUR CLEANUP PROJECT

Our project is _____.

We will need to contact Mr./Ms. _____

to get permission to do our project.

Our project date will be _____.

Our project will take _____ hours to complete.

We will need these supplies:
- Gloves
- Trash bags
- Safety or other protective clothing, if needed
- Water
- First-aid kit
- Safety glasses
- Sun protection

4A

_____   _____
Date   Den Leader's OK

REQUIREMENT 4B | Participate in a patriotic community parade or other civic event that honors our country.

4B

_____   _____
Date   Den Leader's OK

A BEAR GOES FISHING

BEAR

ELECTIVE ADVENTURE

Complete at least three of the following:

1. Discover and learn about three types of fish in your area. Draw a color picture of each fish, record what each one likes to eat, and describe what sort of habitat each one likes.

2. Learn about your local fishing regulations with your den leader or a parent or guardian. List three of the regulations you learn about and one reason each regulation exists.

3. Learn about fishing equipment, and make a simple fishing pole. Practice casting at a target.

4. Go on a fishing adventure, and spend a minimum of one hour trying to catch a fish. Put into practice the things you have learned about fish and fishing equipment.

SNAPSHOT OF ADVENTURE

Grizzly bears in the wild use their fishing skills to catch good, nutritious food. After you complete this adventure, you'll be able to do the same thing. You won't have to use your paws, however! Instead, you'll use a cane pole or a rod and reel. You'll also learn about the fish that live nearby and the rules that good fishermen follow. And who knows? You may discover a hobby that you can enjoy for years to come. So grab your tackle, and let's go fishing!

COMPLETE AT LEAST THREE OF THE FOLLOWING:

REQUIREMENT 1 | **Discover and learn about three types of fish in your area. Draw a color picture of each fish, record what each one likes to eat, and describe what sort of habitat each one likes.**

Do you know someone who is a picky eater? (Maybe it's you!) Do you have friends who really hate cold weather or who love being out in the sun?

Fish can be the same way. Some species of fish will eat just about anything; others are pickier. Some like cold water; others like warm water. Some live in fresh water (inland lakes and rivers); others live in salt water (oceans and shoreline areas). Some like to hide in underwater brush piles; others like to swim in open water.

Before you go fishing, it is important to know about the fish that live in your area. Learn about three fish species that live in your local waters. Record what you discovered on these pages.

 You can find links to state fish and wildlife agencies on the internet (with permission) at **www.fws.gov/offices/**.

You can learn about fish species at your school or local library or on the internet with the help of your parent or guardian. Your state has a government agency that takes care of the fish population. It can be a good source for information about fish species.

Some communities have fish hatcheries (places that grow fish eggs) that you can tour and where you can learn about fish.

Other good sources of information are local fishing clubs and stores that sell fishing equipment and bait.

FISH IN MY AREA

Fish Species 1: _____

Looks Like:

Likes to Eat: _____

Habitat: _____

Fish Species 2: _____

Looks Like:

Likes to Eat: _____

Habitat: _____

Fish Species 3: _____

Looks Like:

Likes to Eat: _____

Habitat: _____

1

REQUIREMENT 2 | Learn about your local fishing regulations with your den leader or a parent or guardian. List three of the regulations you learn about and one reason each regulation exists.

There are rules to follow when fishing. These rules (which are sometimes called regulations) are important because they help protect the fish and the environment they live in. It is important that you learn these rules, understand what they mean, and promise to obey them. A Scout is obedient!

Your local area may have rules about where and when you can fish, how big a fish must be to keep, and how many fish you are allowed to catch and keep. In some places you must put the fish you catch back in the water. This practice is called catch and release. It is a good way to make sure fish can continue to live in the place you are fishing. There may also be rules about the use of live bait.

FISHING REGULATIONS

Fishing Regulation 1: _____

This regulation is important because _____

_____

Fishing Regulation 2: _____

This regulation is important because _____

_____

Fishing Regulation 3: _____

This regulation is important because _____

_____

Your state probably has a license requirement, meaning that people must apply for a fishing license before they go fishing. Cub Scout–age fishermen often don't have to have a license, but be sure to find out about licensing requirements in your area.

In addition to your state and local fishing laws, there are also some "good neighbor" rules that are important for you to follow.

+ Always ask permission before fishing on another person's property. (A Scout is courteous.)

+ Always leave the area cleaner than you found it. Take along a trash bag for any trash you find. (A Scout is clean.)

+ Always let an adult know where you are going and when you will be back. (A Scout is trustworthy.)

+ Always fish with a buddy.

+ Do not intrude on a spot where others are already fishing, which can scare away fish. (A Scout is friendly.)

+ Do not fish in a swimming area. People might step on lost hooks.

+ Decide with your parent or guardian whether you should wear a life jacket while fishing. (A Scout is obedient.)

+ Check the weather forecast before you go fishing and watch the weather while you are fishing. Never fish when lightning is striking in the area or when there is a possibility of flooding.

+ Be sure the place you choose to fish is safe. Things to watch for include slippery rocks, a steep bank that goes to the water's edge, unclean water, debris left from previous high water, and a swiftly moving current.

Be sure to discuss any other rules your family has so you will be safe while fishing.

2

Date   Den Leader's OK

There are many ways to catch fish. You can use a fishing pole, a rod and reel, or a net. Some fishermen even use their bare hands!

FISHING POLE

The simplest way to catch fish is with a fishing pole.
To make a fishing pole, you will need:

- A sturdy stick, 4 to 5 feet long
- Fishing line
- Scissors
- A fishhook

You could use your hiking stick for your fishing pole, but the best type of wood to use is something that is strong but flexible. Bamboo that is about a half inch thick is a good choice.

Tie one end of the fishing line to one end of the pole. If one end of the pole is bigger than the other, tie the line to the bigger end. Now, wrap the line in a spiral around the pole until you reach the tip. Tie the line firmly to the tip, but don't cut the line. Instead, measure out more line so you have a piece hanging down that is a foot or so longer than the pole.

That line you wrapped around the pole will help you if you catch a fish so big it breaks your pole in two. Even though the pole is broken, you will still have captured the fish!

Cut off the line and tie a fishhook on the end. To prevent injuries, stick the hook's barb into the bottom of the pole until you get to your fishing spot. Then, bait the hook, and you're ready go fishing.

Just hang your pole out over the water and lower the bait. Once a fish is on the hook, jerk the line out of the water and grab your fish.

ROD AND REEL

It's fun to fish with a simple fishing pole, but most fishermen use a rod and reel instead. This equipment lets you cast your line farther out in the water. And when you hook a fish, it's easy to reel it in. Here are the pieces you will need.

Rod. The rod takes the place of the fishing pole. It has eyelets (metal rings) along its length that fishing line runs through. Most rods are made of fiberglass or synthetic material like carbon fiber.

Some come apart so you can transport them easily; these are called take-down rods.

The weight of rods varies. To catch small fish, you could use an ultralight rod. To catch fish like trout, you would use a long, thin lightweight rod called a fly rod. For bigger fish, you would need a rod that is bigger around and stronger. If you were going deep-sea fishing, you might use a rod that's 20 feet long!

Reel. The reel connects to the rod near its handle. Inside the reel is a spool that your fishing line wraps around (and around and around and around). From the reel, the end of the line goes up the pole through the eyelets before you add your hook or lure. To reel in the line, you turn a handle. To let the line go when you are casting (tossing your line out on the water), you release a trigger.

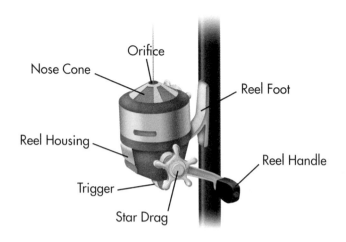

There are many types of reels. As a new fisherman, you might want to pick a close-faced reel that has a cover to protect the line inside. Open-faced or spincasting reels don't have a cover and take more skill to use. Without practice, you can end up with something called a "bird's nest": a big knotted wad of fishing line that is no longer usable.

FISHING LINE

There are many types and colors of fishing line. Some line is meant to catch fish that weigh only 2 pounds. Some is meant to catch fish that weigh 10, 20, or even 50 or more pounds. Be sure to use line that is strong enough for the fish you want to catch. Otherwise, a fish can break the line and get away.

BAIT

You will also need to have the correct bait for the type of fish you are fishing for. If the fish don't like to eat the bait you are using, they won't bite. Do you remember what you learned in requirement 1 about the fish in your area?

You will need to decide if you want to use live bait like minnows, worms, or crickets or if you want to use artificial bait. There are many types of artificial bait. Some make noise in the water or spin around to attract fish. Some are designed to look like live bait.

One special kind of artificial bait is a fishing fly. This is a lure that looks like a real fly. It sits on top of the water waiting for fish to come up and bite. Some fishermen tie their own flies. If you are good with your hands, you might try tying your own flies one day.

TACKLE BOX

A tackle box is a good place to store your bait and other fishing supplies (called tackle) while you are traveling and while you are fishing. It keeps your tackle clean and organized.

You can buy a tackle box at a store or reuse something you find around your home. Be sure there is a way to secure the lid so it doesn't open at the wrong time!

Here are some things to carry in your tackle box:

- ◆ Artificial bait   ◆ Hooks
- ◆ Scissors

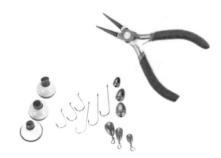

◆ Bobbers   ◆ Needle-nose pliers   ◆ Sinkers

Bobbers are small floats that attach to your fishing line and keep your hook at a certain level.

Sinkers let you fish lower in the water because they pull down on the hook.

Barbless hooks cause less harm to a fish's mouth when you are practicing catch-and-release fishing. If you cannot find barbless hooks, you can use pliers to flatten the barbs on regular hooks.

Pliers help you remove hooks from fish and pull knots tight.

Scissors let you cut off fishing line after you tie it on a hook.

CUB SCOUT SIX ESSENTIALS

◆ First-aid kit   ◆ Flashlight   ◆ Sun protection
◆ Filled water bottle   ◆ Trail food   ◆ Whistle

It is also a good idea to carry the Cub Scout Six Essentials when you go fishing. Other items to carry include raingear and a life jacket.

Fishing can be an expensive hobby, but it doesn't have to be. If you want to learn about fishing but aren't sure whether you will like it, you may be able to borrow some equipment from a family member or friend. Once you decide you like it, you can purchase the proper equipment. You can also buy one or two items at a time and slowly build up a collection of fishing gear.

FISHING KNOTS

You must know the proper types of knots for tying hooks to your line. Because fishing line is stiff and slippery, you can't just use a regular knot. You need a knot that will jam against itself and hold tight. Here are two good knots to learn.

Improved clinch knot. Run the end of the line through the eye of the hook, double the line back, and make six twists around

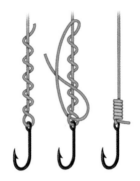

the standing part (the long part of the line). Run the end of the line through the small loop where the line joins the eye and then back through the large loop you just formed. Partially close the knot and moisten it a little with water before securing it tightly against the hook eye.

Palomar knot. Double the line to make a 4- to 6-inch loop, then pass the end of the loop through the eye. (You may need to crimp the end of the loop so it will go through the eye.) Tie a loose overhand knot in the doubled line. Pass the hook through the loop and pull on the doubled line to tighten the knot, guiding the loop over the top of the eye. Cut off the short end of the line.

CASTING

To practice casting, you will need a rod with a reel attached. Instead of using a hook, tie a sinker on your line so it will be heavy enough to cast.

Place a target, and practice hitting the target with the sinker. Do this until you can get closer to the target than you were at first.

As your accuracy improves, move farther from the target. The time you spend practicing will help make fishing safe and fun.

3

_____   _____
Date   **Den Leader's OK**

REQUIREMENT 4 | Go on a fishing adventure, and spend a minimum of one hour trying to catch a fish. Put into practice the things you have learned about fish and fishing equipment.

It is fun to practice casting and to pick out fishing gear, but the real fun happens when you actually go fishing. Nothing is as exciting as watching your bobber disappear under the water or feeling the pull on your line as you reel in a big fish! Make a plan with your den or your parent or guardian for where and when you'll go fishing.

Spend a minimum of one hour trying to catch a fish. Remember all the

things you have learned about fish, fishing equipment, and the rules of fishing. And remember that a Scout is cheerful—even if you don't catch a fish.

4

_____
Date

_____
Den Leader's OK

BEAR PICNIC BASKET

ELECTIVE ADVENTURE

Complete at least three of the following:

1. Create your own Bear cookbook using at least five recipes you might cook or prepare either on your own or with some adult help. Include at least one recipe each for breakfast, lunch, dinner, and a nutritious snack.

2. With a family member or den leader, prepare for cooking by explaining the importance of planning, tool selection, sanitation, and cooking safety.

3. Select and prepare two nutritious snacks for yourself, your family, or your den.

4. With the help of an adult, select a recipe to prepare in a kitchen for your den or your family. Help to select the needed ingredients, perhaps from a garden, grocery store, or farmers' market. Cook and serve your planned meal. Clean up after the preparation and cooking.

5. With the help of an adult, select a recipe to prepare in the outdoors for your family or den. Help to select the needed ingredients, perhaps from a garden, grocery store, or farmers' market. Cook and serve your planned meal. Clean up after the preparation and cooking.

SNAPSHOT OF ADVENTURE

When your stomach growls like a bear, you know it is time to eat. In this adventure, you will get to eat some yummy food that you create yourself. You will learn how to cook at home and at a camp, and you will even put together your own Bear cookbook to record your favorite recipes. Cooking is a lot of fun, so go wash your paws and let's get busy in the kitchen!

COMPLETE AT LEAST THREE OF THE FOLLOWING:

REQUIREMENT 1 | Create your own Bear cookbook using at least five recipes you might cook or prepare either on your own or with some adult help. Include at least one recipe each for breakfast, lunch, dinner, and a nutritious snack.

How does a new chef get started? With a recipe, of course! There are many places you can look for recipes. Here are some of them.

Family. Ask your family members about things they like to cook. Some families hand down recipes from generation to generation. Your parents or grandparents may have cookbooks they have used for many years that you can borrow.

People from other countries. Do you have friends and neighbors who came to the United States from other countries? Do you have family members who live in another part of the world? Different cultures often have very different styles of food that are fun to try.

The library. Your local library probably has cookbooks you can borrow. You may even find cookbooks designed just for kids like you.

Newspapers. Many newspapers have a food section with recipes.

Magazines. Ask your family, neighbors, or other adults you know if they have magazines with recipes you can look through.

Television. There are several TV networks that have shows dedicated to food and recipes.

The internet. With the help of an adult, you can research recipes on the internet. You'll be surprised at how many different recipes you can find for the same food item!

Food packages. Check cereal and baking mix boxes for recipe suggestions.

Other Cub Scouts. Ask your friends what they like to eat and how they cook it. You can exchange recipes with your friends.

You! You can create your own recipes by experimenting with flavors, seasonings, and cooking methods. Start with a few basic ingredients, and then add other ingredients to make your recipe. Be sure to keep notes as you are creating so you will remember what you did. Don't be afraid to try new things!

After you have gathered your recipes, put them in a book that you can use at home or take on a campout. One way to do that is to write each recipe on a 4-by-6-inch index card. Make front and back covers out of heavy cardboard. Punch two holes along the upper edge of each card and each cover, then use string or a shoelace to tie the book together. (Be sure the holes are in the same places on each card.) Cover the front and back with fabric and glue, stickers, or your own original artwork.

Apple Crisp
Serves: 8
Cooking Time: 35 minutes
8 apples, peeled
1 ½ cups brown sugar
1 cup flour
1 cup oats
1 teaspoon cinnamon
1 teaspoon nutmeg
½ cup cold butter
1 tablespoon lemon juice

Apple Crisp

Serves: 8
Cooking Time: 35 minutes

Ingredients:
8 apples, peeled and sliced
1½ cups brown sugar
1 cup flour
1 cup oats
1 teaspoon cinnamon
1 teaspoon nutmeg
½ cup cold butter
1 tablespoon lemon juice

Instructions:
Preheat oven to 375 degrees. Mix the apples with
the lemon juice until well coated. (The lemon juice
keeps the apples from turning brown.) Spray
a 13-by-9-inch baking dish with cooking
spray. Spread the apples in the bottom
of the dish. Mix the remaining ingredients
together in a medium-sized bowl
until crumbly. Spread over the
apples. Bake at 375 degrees
for 35 minutes.

! Any time a member of your den is injured, tell an adult first.

COOKING FIRST AID

MINOR BURN OR SCALD

A burn happens when your skin touches something hot. A scald happens when your skin comes in contact with hot steam. Both can be painful and need some first-aid attention.

If the skin is unbroken, run cool water over the area of the burn or soak it in cool water (not ice water). Keep the area under the water for at least five minutes. A clean, cold, wet towel will also help reduce pain. Show the burned area to an adult.

MINOR CUT

Small cuts in the skin can allow bacteria to enter the body and cause infection. Wash minor cuts with soap and water. Apply antibiotic ointment and cover with a dry, sterile dressing or an adhesive bandage to help prevent infection and protect the wound. Before applying a bandage, show the cut to an adult. Clean and rebandage wounds each day. If the cut is more serious, get help from an adult immediately. Taking proper care of a wound will help prevent other health issues like an infection.

_____   _____
Date   Den Leader's OK

REQUIREMENT 2 | With a family member or den leader, prepare for cooking by explaining the importance of planning, tool selection, sanitation, and cooking safety.

You've collected your recipes and you're ready to roll, right? Before you start opening packages and mixing ingredients, you need to understand a few things. These things will help you be the best cook you can be.

PLANNING

Do these things first:

♦ Decide what you want to cook, and find a recipe.

♦ Read the recipe all the way to the end. Now read it again. Make sure you have plenty of time and you understand what to do. If the recipe is hard to understand, ask for help.

♦ Check your pantry and refrigerator to make sure you have all the ingredients you need. It's hard to make a peanut butter and jelly sandwich if you don't have any peanut butter!

♦ Check your pans and utensils to make sure they are clean and that you have the right ones. Some recipes call for special tools, such as cookie cutters or a mixer.

♦ Consider food allergies. If you are cooking for other people, ask them about any food allergies they have so you don't prepare something that will make them sick.

♦ Wash your hands and make sure your work surfaces are clean. Wipe down surfaces with soapy water and rinse them off.

A Scout is clean. Food safety is the most important part of cooking. It's even more important than dessert!

COOKING TOOLS

Depending on what you are going to cook, you may need some of these tools.

Kitchen spoon. This is a large version of the spoon you eat cereal with. Some have slots in the bowl to drain liquid.

Whisk. This tool lets you whip egg whites or scramble eggs.

Hand mixer or electric mixer. These tools make it easier to mix ingredients.

Blender or food processor. This tool mixes liquids together. It may also have a setting to chop ingredients.

Kitchen knife. This tool is used to cut up ingredients like fruit and vegetables.

Measuring cups. These tools let you measure ingredients. When a recipe calls for 2 cups of flour or a half cup of milk, grab your measuring cups.

Measuring spoons. These tools are similar to measuring cups, but they measure small amounts like teaspoons and tablespoons.

COOKING TERMS

Here are some words you may see in recipes.

Stir. Combine ingredients until they look smooth and are all one color. Batters (cake, cupcake, pancake, etc.) should usually not be lumpy, but check the recipe to be sure.

Mix. Combine wet ingredients (eggs, milk, butter, etc.) and dry ingredients (flour, salt, baking soda, etc.) to form a batter. You can do this with a whisk or a mixer.

Beat. Mix quickly to make the mixture smooth and light.

Blend. Make a very smooth liquid with no lumps. The mixture should look like a runny milkshake or smoothie.

Chop. Cut ingredients into smaller pieces with a knife on a cutting board. Ask for help from an adult with this so you don't cut yourself.

Bake. Cook the food in an oven. Preheat the oven to the right temperature before putting the food in. An adult can help you with this step.

Fry, sauté, or brown. Cook something in a skillet on the stovetop. Heat a little oil in the pan first to keep the food from sticking. An adult can help you with this step.

COOKING SAFETY

Stoves and ovens can cause serious burns, steam from pots can scald your skin, and sharp tools can cause cuts. Also, if you handle food the wrong way, people can get sick. Follow these rules to keep yourself and the people who will eat your food safe.

* Request permission to use the kitchen, and know your family's safety rules before using anything in the kitchen.
* Have a first-aid kit nearby in case you hurt yourself.
* Ask an adult for help when you need to use a knife, the stovetop, the oven, or any electrical appliance.
* Wear shoes in case you drop a heavy pan or a glass bowl or measuring cup.
* Keep work surfaces and your hands clean. Wash your hands before you start cooking, after you handle raw meat, and when you are done cooking.
* Clean up your pots and pans, utensils, and work surfaces once you have finished. Wash your dishes or place them in the dishwasher.

When you join a troop, you will work with your patrol (which is similar to a den) to plan your meals, do the shopping, and prepare and cook them as a group.

RECIPE CHANGES

Sometimes you will need to change a recipe to make it work for you. Let's say you have a recipe for one apple crisp but you need to double the size. You can use math skills to change the recipe.

Use your math skills to change this recipe.

APPLE CRISP

Recipe for One Apple Crisp	x 2 =	Doubled Recipe
8 apples		_____ apples
1½ cups of brown sugar		_____ cups of brown sugar
1 cup of flour		_____ cups of flour
1 cup of oats		_____ cups of oats
1 teaspoon of cinnamon		_____ teaspoons of cinnamon
1 teaspoon of nutmeg		_____ teaspoons of nutmeg
½ cup of cold butter		_____ cup of cold butter
1 tablespoon of lemon juice		_____ tablespoons of lemon juice

See how easy that was? You can use the same math to prepare enough snacks for your entire den. You can also divide everything if the recipe will make more food than you need.

That's not the only kind of change you can make. If you don't like apples, you can substitute peaches. If you like nuts or raisins, you can add those too.

Usually, it's a good idea to follow a recipe exactly the first time you make it. The next time, try some small changes. Make a note of your changes so you can remember them in the future.

2

_____   _____
Date   **Den Leader's OK**

REQUIREMENT 3 | Select and prepare two nutritious snacks for yourself, your family, or your den.

Nutritious snacks can give you a boost of energy between meals. There are lots of great snacks that you can make with little or no help from an adult.

Here are some examples:

+ Nuts (pecans, walnuts, peanuts, etc.)

+ Fresh fruit, dried fruit, fruit juice

+ Raw vegetables (carrots, celery, broccoli, cauliflower, green peppers)

+ Cheese

+ Yogurt

+ Popcorn

+ Peanut butter

+ Milk

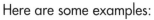

You can eat these snacks by themselves or put them together to create something even better.

Here are some examples:

+ Cream cheese and jelly on graham crackers and a glass of milk

+ Sliced apple with peanut butter or cheese

+ Dried fruit mixed with your choice of nuts

+ Raw vegetables or sliced fruit dipped in yogurt

+ Celery with peanut butter and raisins

None of these snacks have to be cooked, so they are easy to prepare. However, you do need to remember the kitchen safety rules you learned. You should also wash raw vegetables and fruits with skin on them before you eat them.

These ideas are just the beginning. Put on your chef's hat and see how creative you can be in making snacks that taste great and are good for you, too.

The two nutritious snacks I selected and prepared were:

Snack _____ prepared for _____.

Snack _____ prepared for _____.

3 _____   _____
            Date   **Den Leader's OK**

You can choose all sorts of food items to prepare at home. **Here are some examples:**

Breakfast: French toast or scrambled eggs

Lunch: Tuna, chicken salad, or grilled cheese sandwich

Dinner: Spaghetti with sauce or tacos

Pick one of these items or something else to prepare. Talk with everyone about how they liked what you cooked and decide what you would do differently next time.

I cooked _____ Date _____

You may decide you want to make changes to your recipe the next time. Maybe there wasn't enough food to go around. Maybe the food was too spicy (or not spicy enough). Write down the changes you would make so you remember them next time.

Finally, be sure to clean up the kitchen and all the pots, pans, and utensils you used. Remember that a Scout is clean! In many ways, cooking outdoors is just like cooking indoors. You can really cook anything at camp that you can cook at home.

But there are some additional questions to think about. What will the cooking source be? Will it be charcoal in a fire ring, a grill, or a camping stove? (All of these methods require the help of an adult.) Is there water nearby for easy cleanup? How will you get the food to the cooking site? How do you need to adjust the cooking times and methods?

Here are some ideas for each meal:
Breakfast – Oatmeal or pancakes

Lunch – Grilled hot dogs or soup

Dinner – Foil dinner or English
muffin pizza (see the
recipes on the next page)

ENGLISH MUFFIN PIZZA

You will need one English muffin split into two pieces. Spread pizza sauce on both halves, cover with cheese, and add any ingredient that you like to the top. Place your pizzas on a piece of

heavy-duty foil and turn the edges of the foil up, or place them in a pan covered with foil. Have an adult help you place the foil on a heated grill. Watch carefully. Once the cheese has melted, your pizza should be ready to eat.

FOIL DINNER

Cooking in foil packs is a fun way to cook meat, vegetables, and even fruit over hot coals. Plus, the cleanup is easy!

Start with a square piece of heavy-duty aluminum foil. A square sheet that is the width of the roll will work fine. Lay the foil shiny side up on a table, and smear a little butter or margarine on it.

Put a hamburger patty on the foil, and then add sliced potatoes, carrots, onions, broccoli, or whatever else sounds good. The vegetables should all be cut to about the same thickness to help them all cook evenly. Season with salt, pepper, garlic salt, or your favorite herbs. Sprinkle with a little water, maybe two or three teaspoons full. Fold the foil edges up over the food. Fold them down once, crease gently, then fold down again and crease.

Now, do the same thing with the open ends of the foil pack. The idea is to seal the moisture in the package. Try not to rip the seams, but if you do, finish wrapping, then repeat with another layer of foil. Cook the foil pack for 20 to 30 minutes over white-hot coals, turning once. Ask an adult to take the foil pack off the coals. Be careful when you open the foil pack because a lot of steam will come out.

FOIL COOKING TIMES

You can cook many foods in foil packs. Here are approximate cooking times for some of them. The depth of the charcoal bed, the temperature of the food, and the size of the food will affect cooking times.

♦ Hamburger: **15–20 minutes**
♦ Chicken pieces: **20–30 minutes**
♦ Hot dogs: **5–10 minutes**
♦ Pork chops: **30–40 minutes**
♦ Carrots: **15–20 minutes**
♦ Ears of corn: **6–10 minutes**
♦ Whole potatoes: **45–60 minutes**
♦ Potato slices: **10–15 minutes**
♦ Whole apples: **20–30 minutes**

4

Date

Den Leader's OK

BEAT OF THE DRUM

ELECTIVE ADVENTURE

Complete requirement 1 plus two others from requirements 2–4.

1. Learn about the history and culture of American Indians or other indigenous people who lived in your area long ago.

2. Create a legend by building a diorama, writing a story, or presenting a skit.

3. Complete one of the following:

   A. Make a dream catcher.

   B. Make a craft similar to one made by American Indians or indigenous people.

   C. Make a drum. Once your drum is complete, create a ceremonial song.

4. Complete one of the following:

   A. Visit an Order of the Arrow dance ceremony.

   B. Visit an American Indian event or an event presented by other indigenous people.

   C. Learn and demonstrate ceremonial dance steps.

   D. Create a ceremonial dance.

SNAPSHOT OF ADVENTURE

Most Americans have ancestors who came here from other parts of the world. But American Indians have always been here—or at least they've been here since around 12,000 B.C., which is a long, long time ago!

American Indian culture is an important part of our country's traditions. In this adventure, you will learn about American Indian tribes in your area and about customs like crafts, music, and dancing. You'll also get a chance to make some of these traditions your own.

COMPLETE REQUIREMENT 1 PLUS TWO OTHERS FROM REQUIREMENTS 2-4.

REQUIREMENT 1 | **Learn about the history and culture of American Indians or other indigenous people who lived in your area long ago.**

When Christopher Columbus first came to North America in 1492, people had already been living here for thousands of years. These American Indians lived off the land, planting crops and hunting for food. They also did some pretty amazing things, like building huge pyramids in Mexico, developing new types of crops, and inventing the number zero.

Why are the native peoples of the United States often called American Indians? At first, Christopher Columbus thought he'd sailed all the way around the world and reached India.

Groups of American Indians with similar family backgrounds and cultures are referred to as tribes, and there are many of them. Today, the United States government recognizes more than 500 tribes. Every tribe is unique, but history and customs are very important to all of them.

For this requirement, see what you can learn about the American Indians who lived in your area before the European explorers arrived. Did they stay in one place or move around all the time? Did they hunt, fish, or grow crops? Were they peaceful or warlike? Do they still have a presence in your part of the country? Do any cities or rivers in your area have names based on their words?

MY AMERICAN INDIAN NEIGHBORS

One tribe that lived or lives in my area:

_____

What I learned about them: _____

_____

_____

Date _____   **Den Leader's OK** _____

A legend is a story that is passed down from generation to generation. Some legends tell about famous characters like King Arthur or people like Pocahontas. Others explain why things are a certain way. American Indian tribes have legends that they have preserved for thousands of years.

Here is a legend from the Cherokee tribe that explains how the Milky Way galaxy came to be:

> Once upon a time, there weren't many stars in the sky. In those days, people grew a lot of corn, which they dried and turned into cornmeal. One day, the people in a Cherokee village discovered that something had stolen some of their cornmeal. They saw dog prints around the bag. The prints were huge, far too big to be from an ordinary dog. The elders of the village said it must be a spirit dog.
>
> That night, the people all got together to guard their cornmeal. After darkness fell, the spirit dog swooped down from the sky and began to eat some cornmeal. The villagers chased the dog away with noisemakers and loud shouts. It ran out of the village, up a hill, and leaped into the sky. As it flew across the sky, kernels of cornmeal fell out of its mouth and became the stars of the Milky Way.

For this requirement, make up your own legend. It could explain how something came to be, like the Cherokee story does. Or it could be based on something that happened in your family a long time ago. It could even describe how a character you admire visited your town.

2

_____ _____
Date   Den Leader's OK

154 ▪ Bear

REQUIREMENT 3A | Make a dream catcher.

Long ago, the Ojibwe (pronounced o-JIB-way) people created dream catchers to hang over the beds of people who were sleeping, especially children. They believed that the night air held dreams, both good ones and bad ones. The dream catcher would let good dreams get through to the sleepers. Bad dreams would be caught in the dream catcher's web and would disappear at daybreak.

Other tribes adopted the dream catcher. Today, many people see the dream catcher as a symbol of American Indians across the country.

A dream catcher has three main parts: a round ring, a web of thread that looks like a spider's web, and feathers. You can imagine good dreams sliding down the feathers onto the sleeper.

DREAM CATCHER

Materials and Tools

- ◆ Paper plate
- ◆ Scissors
- ◆ About 7 feet of yarn
- ◆ Hole punch
- ◆ Beads
- ◆ Feathers

Instructions

1. Using the scissors, cut out the center of the plate so you have a ring that's about 2 inches wide.

2. Using the hole punch, punch holes every inch or so around the ring.

3. Cut a piece of yarn about 5 feet long. Tie one end of the yarn to one of the holes you just made. Run the other end through one of the holes on the other side of the ring and pull it snug (but not so snug that it warps the ring).

4. Keep weaving the yarn between all the holes. Along the way, you can string beads on to the yarn if you like.

5. When you get to the end of the yarn, tie it off in the nearest hole.

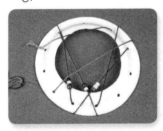

6. Cut three pieces of yarn 5 inches long. Tie a feather to one end of each piece. Tie the other end of each piece to a hole on the bottom of the ring. (Punch extra holes if you need to.)

7. Cut one more piece of yarn about 5 inches long. Run it through a hole at the top of the ring and tie it in a knot to form a loop. Use this loop to hang your dream catcher on the wall or from the ceiling.

3A

_____ _____
Date   **Den Leader's OK**

Crafts are a very important part of American Indian culture (and many other cultures). Crafts are pretty to look at, but they also record history, show which tribe someone belongs to, and meet daily needs like providing clothing and shelter. American Indian crafts include beadwork, baskets, cornhusk dolls, moccasins, totem poles, rattles, rain sticks, and more.

For this requirement, pick a craft and make it. You can find ideas for crafts from your library or the internet with the help of an adult.

 There are also kits available from many sources, including your local Scout shop and the **ScoutStuff.org** website.

A talking stick is an easy craft to make. American Indians in many parts of the country have used talking sticks for centuries. During special meetings, a talking stick helps speakers take turns and encourages respectful listening.

TALKING STICK

Materials and Tools

* Stick or dowel rod, approximately one-half inch by 24 inches
* Yarn
* Scraps of felt or fur
* Leather or suede cord
* Craft glue
* Scissors
* Jingle bells, pony beads, feather, or shells

Instructions

1. Cut a piece of 1-inch-by-2-inch felt.
2. Wrap it around the end of the stick. Glue it in place.

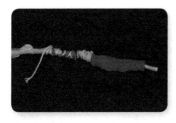

3. Wrap yarn tightly around the stick, adding more glue as needed. Cover about 5 inches of the stick, changing color if desired.

4. Tie the suede lace near the bottom of the yarn wrap. Thread the lace through bells, beads, feathers, or shells to decorate it as you want. Then knot the lace again.

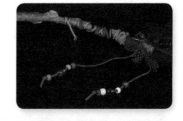

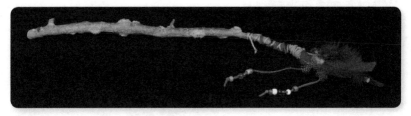

3B

_____ _____
Date   **Den Leader's OK**

REQUIREMENT 3C | Make a drum. Once your drum is complete, create a ceremonial song.

Drums are very important in many American Indian ceremonies and ceremonial dances. In some tribes, several drummers will gather around a big drum and hit it all at the same time as they sing. Dancers move in time with the rhythm of the drum, which represents the heartbeat of the American Indian people.

Authentic American Indian drums are usually made of wooden frames or hollow logs covered with animal skin. You can make your own drum out of a large empty container like a coffee can or oatmeal canister. Cover the outside with construction paper and decorate it. Work with your den leader or family to choose a material to stretch across the opening and attach. Make up your own song to sing as you beat your drum.

3C

_____   _____
Date   **Den Leader's OK**

COMPLETE ONE OF THE FOLLOWING:

REQUIREMENT 4A | Visit an Order of the Arrow dance ceremony.

Many groups work to preserve American Indian traditions. One of them is the Order of the Arrow, which is the national honor society of the Boy Scouts of America. Many Order of the Arrow lodges have ceremony teams and dance teams that study and preserve the traditions of specific tribes. They often perform at camporees, summer camps, Cub Scout pack meetings, and other Scouting events.

Some communities also have powwows where American Indians and people who want to learn about their culture get together. Powwows usually include dancing, ceremonies, craft demonstrations, and traditional food.

To find out about powwows in your area, check with local parks, museums, and cultural centers.

 The **PowWows.com** website, which you can visit with help from an adult, includes a calendar of powwows across the United States and Canada.

 4A

Date   Den Leader's OK

REQUIREMENT 4B | Visit an American Indian event or an event presented by other indigenous people.

The event I attended: _____

What I learned: _____

4B

Date   Den Leader's OK

REQUIREMENT 4C | Learn and demonstrate ceremonial dance steps.

Ceremonial dancing is an important part of American Indian culture. Some dances have religious significance. Some re-enact great events in a tribe's history. Some celebrate successful hunts, harvests, or important times like the summer solstice (the longest day of the year).

Talk with a member of the Order of the Arrow or someone at an American Indian powwow. Find out about the dancing that they do. Learn about the significance of the dances. Learn a few dance steps.

 A Scout is courteous. Always show respect when you learn about the traditions of a group of people.

4C

_____   _____
Date   Den Leader's OK

REQUIREMENT 4D | Create a ceremonial dance.

Some American Indian dances express thanks for good things that have happened. For this requirement, create a ceremonial dance to give thanks for something special to you. You could even make a ceremonial costume to wear during your dance. Have a friend or family member create a beat on the drum you made.

4D

Date

Den Leader's OK

CRITTER CARE

ELECTIVE ADVENTURE

Complete all of the following:

1. Do one of the following:

   A. If you have a pet, make a list of tasks that you did to take care of the pet for two weeks.

   B. If you do not have a pet, research one that you would like to have and prepare a report about the care it needs.

2. Complete one of the following:

   A. Make a poster or a PowerPoint presentation about your pet or a pet that you would like to have. Share the poster or presentation with your den, pack, or family.

   B. Make a poster or PowerPoint presentation explaining three ways that animals can help people. Share the poster or presentation with your den, pack, or family.

3. Complete at least one of the following and share with your den, pack, or family:

   A. Visit with a local veterinarian or an animal shelter caretaker. Find out what types of animals he or she might see on a regular basis and the types of care he or she gives to them.

   B. Learn about careers that involve the care of animals. What education, training, and experience are required?

SNAPSHOT OF ADVENTURE

Did you know that two-thirds of Americans have a pet dog, cat, horse, bird, fish, hamster, or other animal? It's true. In fact, there are more pets than people in America!

Pets are fun, but they are also a big responsibility. Pets need food, water, shelter, and exercise in order to stay healthy. When you look after a pet, whether it belongs to you or a neighbor, you learn a lot about love, loyalty, and caring. Learning to look after pets—and having fun with them—is what this adventure is all about.

DO ONE OF THE FOLLOWING:

REQUIREMENT 1A | **If you have a pet, make a list of tasks that you did to take care of the pet for two weeks.**

Does your cat open cans of food when it's hungry? Does your dog take itself for a walk? Of course not! Unlike people, pets can't take care of themselves. They need someone to take care of them.

Every kind of pet needs a clean, dry place to sleep (except for fish, of course!). A dog might have a special place in your home where it sleeps. A horse might live in a barn or out in a pasture. A hamster lives in a cage. A cat will make its own bed in a sunny spot by a window.

Nutritious food, clean water, and plenty of exercise help keep pets healthy. Just like you, your pet will get sick if it eats nothing but junk food and never gets any exercise. Your veterinarian can suggest the right food and exercise for your pet.

Speaking of your veterinarian, most pets need regular checkups.

Your veterinarian can help you make sure your pet stays healthy. He or she can also give your pet vaccinations to prevent serious diseases. Your vet might even clean your pet's teeth.

For this requirement, take care of a pet for two weeks. Write down the things you did.

MY PET

The pet I cared for is a _____ (type of animal).

Its name is _____.

Things I did to care for it:

_____

_____

_____

_____

_____

1A

_____   _____
Date   **Den Leader's OK**

Pets have amazing stories. Did you know that cats can see six times better than humans at night? Did you know that dogs can vary in size from 2 pounds (a Chihuahua) to more than 150 pounds (a Great Dane)? Did you know that hamsters bathe themselves like cats? Did you know that horses produce 10 gallons of sweat a day?

See what you can learn about a pet that you would like to have by reading a book or exploring the internet (with your parent's or guardian's permission). Write down what you learned on this page.

WHAT I LEARNED

_____

_____

_____

_____

1B

_____   _____
Date   Den Leader's OK

REQUIREMENT 2A | Make a poster or a PowerPoint presentation about your pet or a pet that you would like to have. Share the poster or presentation with your den, pack, or family.

Tell other people about your chosen pet by making a poster. You could include pictures, the facts you learned in requirement 1, and something about the toys that your pet or the pet you would like to have likes to play with, or the tricks it can do. If you own the pet, you might also include information about where you got your pet and anything you know about its lineage (its parents and family history).

2A

Date   Den Leader's OK

REQUIREMENT 2B | Make a poster or PowerPoint presentation explaining three ways that animals can help people. Share the poster or presentation with your den, pack, or family.

There are many ways pets can help people. Search-and-rescue crews use dogs to find people who are missing. Guide dogs help blind people get around on their own. Therapy pets help people who are sad or who are dealing with a lot of stress (like kids in the hospital). There are even dogs that can call for help if someone is having a medical emergency.

How have you seen animals at work? Can you think of other ways animals might help people?

HOW ANIMALS HELP PEOPLE

_____

_____

2B

_____   _____
Date   Den Leader's OK

> **REQUIREMENT 3A** | Visit with a local veterinarian or an animal shelter caretaker. Find out what types of animals he or she might see on a regular basis and the types of care he or she gives to them.

A veterinarian is a doctor who takes care of animals. If you have a dog or a cat, you probably already know a veterinarian.

But not all veterinarians take care of family pets. Some take care of farm animals. Some take care of pets in animal shelters. Some even take care of zoo animals. Imagine cleaning a tiger's teeth or taking a giraffe's temperature!

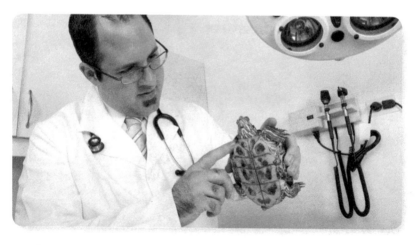

 A Scout is kind. Learning about caring for animals can help you understand what it means to be kind.

Visit with a veterinarian or shelter caretaker in your community. Learn about his or her work and what type of education is required to be a veterinarian. If you like animals, you might decide to become a veterinarian yourself someday.

3A

Date   Den Leader's OK

3B

Date   Den Leader's OK

FORENSICS

ELECTIVE ADVENTURE

Complete all of the following:

1. Talk with your family or den about forensics and how it is used to help solve crimes.

2. Take your fingerprints and learn how to analyze them.

3. Complete one of the following:

   A. Learn about chromatography and how it is used in solving crimes. Do an investigation using different types of black, felt-tip markers. Share your results with your den.

   B. Do an analysis of four different substances: salt, sugar, baking soda, and cornstarch.

4. Complete one of the following:

   A. Visit the sheriff's office or police station in your town. Find out how officers collect evidence.*

   B. Learn about the different jobs available in forensic science. Choose two, and find out what is required to work in those jobs. Share what you learn with your den.

   C. Learn how animals are used to gather important evidence. Talk about your findings with your den

*Note that this may be done during the same visit as "Paws for Action" requirement 3A.

SNAPSHOT OF ADVENTURE

Everywhere you go, you leave behind clues: fingerprints on your juice glass, DNA on your toothbrush, bits of fabric on your favorite chair, and footprints in your yard. Criminals leave behind clues, too. Forensic scientists study those clues to help law enforcement officers solve crimes.

Forensics is all about using science to answer questions about crimes (and other things that have happened). In this adventure, you will get to practice some of the skills of a forensic scientist. You will analyze a fingerprint, a footprint, the contents of ink, and some mysterious white powder. So grab your magnifying glass, and start detecting!

The word "forensics" comes from a Latin word that means to make public. Forensic scientists make information public that was hidden in plain sight.

COMPLETE ALL OF THE FOLLOWING:

REQUIREMENT 1 | Talk with your family or den about forensics and how it is used to help solve crimes.

Thanks to detective stories and crime shows on TV, many people know something about forensics. Talk with the other people in your family and den to find out what they know (or think they know) about forensics.

Write down any questions they have. As you do the other requirements for this adventure, you might be able to answer some of those questions. With an adult's supervision, you can also search the internet for sites that teach about forensics for kids.

Did you know that the Federal Bureau of Investigation (**FBI**) has a site for kids? It's: **www.fbi.gov/fun-games/kids**. Check it out with an adult's permission.

_____ _____
Date   Den Leader's OK

REQUIREMENT 2 | Take your fingerprints and learn how to analyze them.

As you probably know, everybody's fingerprints are unique. Even identical twins have different fingerprint patterns! Police use fingerprints to identify criminals. Fingerprints are also used in other ways, like fingerprint scanners on laptop computers and smartphones.

In this requirement, you will discover what your fingerprints look like. You will need an ink pad and a magnifying glass. Press the tip of one forefinger down on the ink pad so your fingertip is covered with ink. Press that finger straight down in the space below, and then lift it straight up. (If you let it slide around, you will get a smeared print.)

Wait for the ink to dry. Be sure to wash your fingers!

LEFT	RIGHT

Using the magnifying glass, study the print you made. Do the ridges form an arch, a whorl, or a loop? Is the pattern short or tall? Does it lean one way or the other? How does it compare with the prints of others in your den or members of your family?

Arch

Whorl

Loop

_____   _____
Date   Den Leader's OK

178 ▪ Bear

REQUIREMENT 3A | Learn about chromatography and how it is used in solving crimes. Do an investigation using different types of black, felt-tip markers. Share your results with your den.

Chromatography is a big word that means "color writing." It is a technique for separating mixtures of different chemicals. Most chromatography is done in laboratories with expensive equipment, but you can do a simple experiment using materials found around your home. With these materials, you can separate the components of ink.

The pictures on the next page show what your investigation might produce. In this example, several different colors were hidden in the black ink. Chromatography causes the different pigments that make up the black ink to separate and spread out. Each formula used for black ink will create a unique spread of colors.

Forensic scientists do similar investigation on chemicals found at crime scenes. For example, using chromatography, they could identify the type of pen that was used to write a document.

Materials and Tools
  ◆ A coffee filter
  ◆ Several nonpermanent felt-tip markers of different brands
  ◆ A glass of water
  ◆ Scissors
  ◆ Newsprint

Instructions
1. Cut the coffee filter into strips an inch or so wide.

2. Draw a horizontal line across the middle of one of the strips.

3. Put the strip in the glass of water, making sure the line you drew is above the water.

4. Now watch what happens. The coffee filter will slowly absorb water, which will rise toward the top of the strip. As the water rises, it will carry along components of the ink. Lighter components will travel the longest distance; heavier components will not travel very far.

5. When the water nearly reaches the top of the strip (or when you don't see any more changes happening), take the strip out of the water and set it on a piece of newsprint to dry.

Repeat the experiment with several pens. Compare the results to see how similar or different the inks you used are.

3A

_____   _____
Date   **Den Leader's OK**

REQUIREMENT 3B | Do an analysis of four different substances: salt, sugar, baking soda, and cornstarch.

Forensic chemists do other tests to identify unknown substances. For example, they might add a chemical to the substance to see how it changes.

For this requirement you will analyze four common substances: salt, sugar, baking soda, and cornstarch. Use the chart on the next page to keep track of your results.

Do these tests:

* Examine what the substance looks like, with both your naked eye and with a magnifying glass.

* See how it feels when you rub it between your fingers.

* Sniff it to determine how it smells.

* Add a drop of water and, in a different spot, a drop of vinegar. Record how the substance reacts. Does it dissolve? Does it become hard?

	Salt	Sugar	Baking soda	Cornstarch
Appearance (naked eye)				
Appearance (magnifying glass)				
Feel between fingers				
Smell				
Reaction to water				
Reaction with vinegar				

After you've tested all the substances, ask your parent or a friend to give you a sample of one of the substances without telling you what it is. Can you identify it based on your test results?

3B _____ _____
Date **Den Leader's OK**

COMPLETE ONE OF THE FOLLOWING:

REQUIREMENT 4A | Visit the sheriff's office or police station in your town. Find out how officers collect evidence.*

Law enforcement officers collect all sorts of evidence. They interview witnesses. They check security camera videos. And they collect forensic evidence like you've studied about in this adventure.

Visit your local sheriff's office or police station. Find out how law enforcement officers look for and collect evidence.

A Scout is loyal. Learning about how police protect your community can help you understand what it means to be loyal.

*Note that this may be done during the same visit as "Paws for Action" requirement 3A.

4A

_____   _____
Date   Den Leader's OK

There are numerous jobs in the area of forensic science.

Here are a few:

- A medical examiner performs autopsies to determine why people died.
- A toxicologist tests for poisons.
- A fingerprint expert identifies patterns in fingerprints.
- A forensic engineer tries to figure out how a structure collapsed.
- A multimedia scientist looks for clues in surveillance videos and crime-scene photos.

Learn more about two of these jobs or others in the field of forensics. Share what you learned with your den.

4B _____ _____
            Date   **Den Leader's OK**

You probably know that dogs have a really good sense of smell. Because of that, they can be trained to find all sorts of evidence, including blood and drugs that humans might not be able to detect.

Visit the library, explore the internet (with your parent's or guardian's permission), or talk with a law enforcement officer to learn more about how animals are used to gather evidence.

Date   **Den Leader's OK**

GRIN AND BEAR IT

ELECTIVE ADVENTURE

Complete at least four of the following:

1. Play a challenge game or initiative game with the members of your den. Take part in a reflection after the game.

2. Working with the members of your den, organize a Cub Scout carnival and lead it at a special event.

3. Help younger Cub Scouts take part in one of the events at the Cub Scout carnival.

4. After the Cub Scout carnival, discuss with the members of your den and your den leader what went well, what could be done better, and how everyone worked together to make the event a success.

5. With your den, develop a thank-you cheer to recognize those who helped organize the Cub Scout carnival.

SNAPSHOT OF ADVENTURE

The Grin and Bear It adventure is very special because you will be creating and sharing fun! In this adventure, you will play some games with your den, and then you will help plan a Cub Scout carnival for all the other Cub Scouts and their families.

At the carnival, you will have stations where kids and adults can play midway games like Clothespin Ring Toss and Keep Your Balance. You might also do activities like face painting or making balloon animals or maybe have someone demonstrate juggling. Adults and older Scouts might provide snacks and prizes or play music. The Cubmaster will serve as the ringmaster, just like in a big carnival. It's a great way to "grin and bear it"!

REQUIREMENT 1 | Play a challenge game or initiative game with the members of your den. Take part in a reflection after the game.

Lots of games are fun to play. Some also teach you important things. Challenge or initiative games help you learn more about yourself and your friends. They also teach you how to work together as a team. One great thing about these games is that everybody can win!

 A Scout is loyal. Team-building games help you practice being true to the other members of your den.

Here are some games you might play with your den. Your den leader knows other games you can play.

BATTING DOWN THE LINE

Needed: Large indoor or outdoor playing area, any number of players, an inflated balloon

Stand in a line with Scouts about 2 feet apart. On a signal, the first player bats a balloon to the player next to him or her, who bats it to the next player, and so on until the balloon reaches the end of the line. If the balloon touches the ground, a player must take it to the starting line, and the players must begin again.

Two or more dens can play this game at the same time by forming parallel lines.

BLANKET BALL

Needed: Indoor or outdoor area, any number of players, sheet or blanket, playground ball or large soft object

Lay the blanket on the ground and put the ball in the center. The players stand around the blanket, grab its edges, and pick it up. They throw the ball up and catch it by moving the blanket up and down together, trying to get the ball as high as possible.

Two or more dens can play this game. You just need extra blankets and balls. For extra fun, try to toss a ball from one blanket to another and back!

GROUP STAND-UP

Needed: Indoor room or grassy outdoor area, long thick rope (about an inch thick) tied to form a circle

Players sit in a circle holding onto the rope, which is on the ground in front of their feet. Everyone grabs the rope and then pulls gently and evenly on it. If everyone pulls together evenly, the entire group should be able to come to a standing position.

LINE UP

Needed: Any number of players, one blindfold per player or "honor blindfolds" (players promise to keep their eyes closed)

Players are blindfolded and told that no one may talk during the game. The leader asks them to line up by height. When they are done, they should stand in place and remove their blindfolds to see how they did. You can substitute other requirements, such as lining up by shoe size.

You can also play with eyes open. Players cannot talk but can use sign language to communicate. This time they line up by birthday, middle name, number of brothers and sisters they have, or any other direction.

FOREHEAD SQUEEZE RELAY

Needed: Large playing area, even number of players, several tennis balls or other small balls

The object is for two players on each team to carry a ball across the room and back again by holding it between their foreheads. If they drop it, they must start again. When the first pair returns to the starting point, the next pair begins. Keep playing until all players have had a turn. The trick with this game is to see how fast you can move without dropping the ball or orange!

After you play a game, sit down with your den and talk about these questions:

- How did you know you did your best?
- How did you make sure everyone was included?
- How was this game related to the Scout Law?
- How do you know that everyone had fun?
- How would you make the game different next time?
- What did the game teach you about teamwork?

Some games are called feats of skill, while others are played just for fun. You can play these games at a den meeting or choose a few to teach at the Cub Scout carnival.

CLOTHESPIN RING TOSS

Materials: Bucket or wastebasket, clothespins, jar rings

Clamp clothespins around the rim of a bucket or wastebasket. Players stand 10 feet away and try to toss jar rings over the clothespins.

KEEP YOUR BALANCE

Materials: Six- to 8-foot-long two-by-four board, neckerchief for blindfold

Lay the board flat on the ground. One by one, blindfold the players and have them try to walk the length of the board. Anyone who steps off at any point has fallen into the water and is out of the game. If you have more than one team, put boards side by side and have a race.

SMILE

Materials: Coin for flipping

Two teams line up facing each other about 10 feet apart. One team is Heads; the other is Tails. Flip a coin and call it. If heads comes up, the Heads team laughs and smiles while the Tails team members try to keep their faces serious. Any player who laughs at the wrong time switches teams. Then flip the coin again.

MARBLE CHOP SUEY

Materials: Supply of marbles or small candies, several pencils or chopsticks, two dishes for each team

Put six marbles or candies in a small dish. Using two pencils or chopsticks, and using only one hand, players try to move the marbles or candies into a second dish. Using pencils with eraser tips can make this a little easier for younger Scouts. Play this as a skill activity or relay race.

JUGGLER TOSS

Materials: Ball or orange for each player

Pairs of players stand about 5 feet apart in two lines facing each other. Each player has a rubber ball or orange. They toss their balls simultaneously. Score one point for a team when both make the catch. After each catch, they take one step back and repeat. The pair with the most points after a set time limit wins.

1

_____   _____
Date   **Den Leader's OK**

You and your den will help plan and lead a Cub Scout carnival. Other dens may help, and the leaders will help, too. At a den meeting, take turns sharing ideas about what you would like to do at the carnival.

Talk about these things:

* What games and activities will take place at the carnival?

* Who will run each game or activity?

* When and where will the carnival take place?

* How will you tell the other dens about the carnival?

> If the weather will be nice you could have the carnival outside.

It helps to write things down when you plan an activity. You could also draw pictures of how the carnival will look.

Pick an activity to lead. Make a list or draw a picture to show what you need. You might like to work with a friend so that you can practice teaching the activity. This will help you get ready to lead it at the carnival.

Be sure you know what you need to do to get ready for the game you will lead. If you are not sure, ask your den leader or your parent or guardian for help.

2

_____   _____
Date   Den Leader's OK

REQUIREMENT 3 | Help younger Cub Scouts take part in one of the events at the Cub Scout carnival.

When the time for the carnival arrives, your Cubmaster will give a signal and the fun will begin. Everyone will get a chance to try out the games you and your den brought to play.

Your job will be to help younger Cub Scouts or their brothers or sisters take part in one of the activities. The activity may be new to many of the players, so take time to explain how to do it. Demonstrate the activity and answer any questions the players have. And be sure to cheer for them, even if they don't do well at first. If you make sure that they have fun, you will have fun, too.

A Scout is friendly. You can show that you are friendly by being patient and nice with the younger Cub Scouts at your carnival.

3

_____
Date

_____
Den Leader's OK

REQUIREMENT 4 | After the Cub Scout carnival, discuss with the members of your den and your den leader what went well, what could be done better, and how everyone worked together to make the event a success.

Your Cub Scout carnival should be a lot of fun. After all, there will be games and snacks and prizes. Cub Scouts, brothers and sisters, adults, and friends should all have a great time.

But even when events go well, we can learn to do things better. After the Cub Scout carnival is over, talk with your den and your den leader about what you learned.

Talk about these questions:

◆ What games or activities would we repeat next time?

◆ What games or activities would we not do next time?

◆ What games or activities would we add to the carnival next time?

◆ How could we make it better next time?

| 4 | Date | Den Leader's OK |

REQUIREMENT 5 | With your den, develop a thank-you cheer to recognize those who helped organize the Cub Scout carnival.

5

_____ Date

_____ Den Leader's OK

MAKE IT MOVE

ELECTIVE ADVENTURE

Complete all of the following:

1. Create an "exploding" craft stick reaction.

2. Make two simple pulleys, and use them to move objects.

3. Make a lever by creating a seesaw using a spool and a wooden paint stirrer. Explore the way it balances by placing different objects on each end.

4. Complete one of the following:

   A. Draw a Rube Goldberg–type machine. Include at least six steps to complete your action.

   B. Construct a real Rube Goldberg–type machine to complete a task assigned by your den leader. Use at least two simple machines and include at least four steps.

SNAPSHOT OF ADVENTURE

There are lots of ways to do just about anything. Let's say you wanted to put a ball in a cup. The easy way would be to drop it in with your hand. But imagine this solution: You knock over a row of dominos. The last domino bumps into a marble. The marble rolls off a ledge into a bucket that's attached to a pulley. The bucket whizzes down onto a seesaw, causing it to tip. The motion launches a ball from a small cup on the other end of the seesaw into a second, larger cup, which is in just the right place to catch the ball.

Silly? Yes. Fun? Of course!

In this adventure, you'll use your imagination to dream up machines like that. You'll also learn about some important science concepts that make both silly and serious machines work. So put your brain in gear and get ready to make it move!

COMPLETE ALL OF THE FOLLOWING:

REQUIREMENT 1 | Create an "exploding" craft stick reaction.

You can make all sorts of things with craft sticks, but one of the most fun things is a stick "bomb." What you do is weave together a bunch of craft sticks so they form a path around the room. When you pull the first stick out of the weave, all the sticks jump into the air in a chain reaction.

For even more fun, set up a stack of plastic cups at the end of your stick "bomb." The jumping sticks should send the cups flying.

Kids your age and a little bit older have made stick "bombs" with more than 10,000 craft sticks. You don't have to use that many to have fun, however!

All you need for this activity is a bunch of craft sticks. It helps to have two different colors so that you can keep the pattern straight. Or simply draw a line on both sides of half your sticks so you can tell them apart.

If possible, work on a rug or low-pile carpet. The softer surface makes it easier to weave the sticks in and out. Just don't trap any carpet fibers in between your craft sticks.

Here's how to make the weave:

1. Make an X out of two craft sticks, one of each color.

2. Weave in two more sticks, one of each color, using an under/over pattern. The third stick you place should create a tight "V" with the first.

3. As you add new sticks, keep sticks of the same color parallel to each other. The end should stay locked in place by the "V" at the start.

4. Continue weaving as far as you want to go. Always alternate between going under and over, and match up the tips of the sticks.

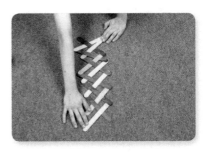

5. You can make turns as you weave; they just have to be gradual. On the outside of the curve, put the tips of each pair of sticks on top of each other. On the inside of the curve, push each new stick in a little farther than before.

6. To lock the end of the stick "bomb" together, add another diagonal stick at the end. When you're ready for an explosion, put a finger on the first

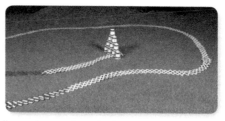

sticks you laid down and pull out the end stick. Let go to start a chain reaction of jumping craft sticks!

Did you notice how weaving the craft sticks together held them in place and how you had to lock them together until you were ready for the explosion? When the sticks are woven together, they have what's called *potential* energy, or energy that is stored up. When they spring apart, they have *kinetic* energy, which is the energy of motion.

How long of a chain reaction were you able to make? Did you knock down a stack of cups? How many cups? Was it easier to do this as a team? What would you do differently next time?

 To see this craft stick activity in action, search for videos on the internet with a parent's or guardian's permission.

_____   _____
Date   **Den Leader's OK**

REQUIREMENT 2 | Make two simple pulleys, and use them to move objects.

A pulley is a simple machine that lets you lift objects into the air. It was invented thousands of years ago but is still used every day. When your den raises a flag on a flagpole, you use a pulley. When a construction crane lifts girders into the air, it uses a pulley. In fact, everything from elevators to workout equipment uses pulleys.

A pulley has just a few parts: a wheel, an axle that the wheel turns around, and a rope or cable. The wheel usually has a groove in it so the rope won't slide off.

Simple pulleys are useful, but what makes them really cool is when you put pulleys together. When you use two pulleys to lift an object, the object becomes twice as easy to lift. When you use four pulleys, it becomes four times as easy to lift. With enough pulleys (and enough really, really strong cable), you could actually lift a car off the ground all by yourself!

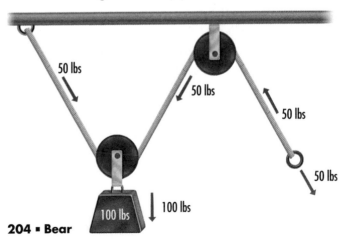

Here are two simple pulleys you can make.

PULLEY #1

Materials

- Rolling pin with handles
- String
- Heavy book

Instructions

1. Wrap the end of the string around the book a couple of times and then tie it snugly.

2. Place the book on the floor and use the string to lift the book with one hand.

3. Now, have a partner hold the rolling pin tightly by the handles at chest height.

4. Loop the string over the top of the rolling pin.

5. Use the string to pull the book up.

Which way of lifting the book was easier? Did one way take more strength than the other?

PULLEY #2

Materials

- Two large spools
- Two pencils or dowels (they must be able to fit in the spool hole and move easily)
- 30 feet of string or strong yarn
- An index card
- A clothespin or clip

Instructions

1. Insert a pencil or dowel into each spool, making sure the spool can spin easily.

2. Tie the two ends of the string or yarn together to form a big loop.

3. Place the loop around the spools.

4. Have a partner hold each of the spool pulleys by its pencil or dowel axle.

5. Stretch your loop until it is tight enough to be straight, but still loose enough to turn.

6. Write a message on a card and attach it to the string with a clothespin near one pulley.

7. Gently pull the string to make the string roll over the spools.

See if you can use your pulley system to deliver a message to a friend on the other side of the room. How else could you use this pulley system? How could you secure the pulleys at both ends so your friends don't have to hold them? What other improvements could you make?

2

_____   _____
         Date   **Den Leader's OK**

What's a lever? That's a fancy term for the science that makes a playground seesaw work. The fulcrum is the hinge or balancing point. The lever is the board.

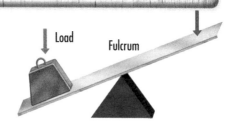

Load   Fulcrum

As you've probably figured out on the playground, if an object is farther from the fulcrum, it takes a smaller force to produce the same work. When you get on the seesaw with someone who's a lot bigger than you, that person has to sit closer to the fulcrum for the seesaw to balance. When you sit very far from the fulcrum, you can lift a heavier person at the other end. (With a really long seesaw, you could even lift a 300-pound football player!)

That principle, called leverage, is why levers are so useful. You can find levers in all sorts of places, including a pair of scissors, a crowbar, a hammer pulling a nail, a wheelbarrow, a bottle opener,

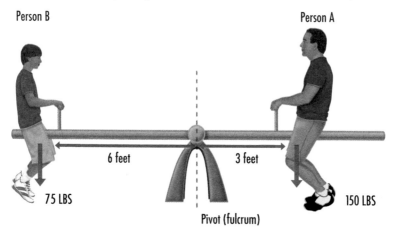

Person B   Person A

6 feet   3 feet

75 LBS   150 LBS

Pivot (fulcrum)

and a nutcracker. (There are three classes of levers, so these things don't all work exactly the same way.)

For this requirement, you will make and experiment with a simple lever.

 A Scout is thrifty. You can try many investigations with simple items from home.

Materials

* Paint stirrer
* Pencil
* Spool (the edges should be wider than the paint stirrer)
* Rubber band
* Small weights or other objects

Instructions

1. Find the middle of the paint stirrer and mark it with the pencil.

2. Hold the spool on the line you just drew.

3. Lay the rubber band over the paint stirrer and loop it over each end of the spool. (This will hold the spool and paint stirrer together.)

Congratulations! You've just made a lever! Now, experiment with it by adding weights or other objects to each end. How easy is it to get the lever to balance? What happens if the weight on one end is too heavy?

After you've played with your lever for a while, move the spool closer to one end of the paint stirrer. How does that change the way the lever works? Do you see why levers can be useful tools?

3

Date   Den Leader's OK

COMPLETE ONE OF THE FOLLOWING:

REQUIREMENT 4A | **Draw a Rube Goldberg–type machine. Include at least six steps to complete your action.**

Rube Goldberg was an amazing inventor, engineer, and cartoonist who lived in the 20th century. He was famous for dreaming up really complicated machines to do simple things like scratching your back or using a napkin.

For this requirement, you will dream up two Rube Goldberg–type machines. The first one will just be on paper, like a Rube Goldberg comic strip, so you can make it as crazy as you want. The second one, which you'll make with your den, should actually work.

MOVE**MAKE IT MOVE ▪ 209**

Here's how to make a Rube Goldberg machine:

1. Choose a simple task like drying your face, putting on a hat, or opening a door.

2. Decide what working elements you want to include. These could include chain reactions, pulleys, levers, ramps, and more.

3. Add your imagination! How could you use those elements in fun ways? How could you include building blocks, toy cars, string, or other items in your design?

4. Draw your first machine on paper. You'll build your second machine with the other members of your den for requirement 4B.

4A

Date	Den Leader's OK

Here are some tips for making a machine with your den:

◆ Keep the task simple. The machine is supposed to be complicated, not the task!

◆ Work together and listen to everyone's ideas.

◆ A Scout is thrifty. Look for things around you that you can use, like craft sticks, marbles, dominos, building blocks, cereal boxes, mailing tubes, yogurt cups, and water bottles.

◆ Avoid anything dangerous (fire, chemicals, mousetraps, etc.).

◆ Build the machine on a drop cloth in case things get messy.

◆ It's OK if your machine doesn't work the first time. A lot of what inventors do is figure out what won't work.

4B _____   _____
     Date   **Den Leader's OK**

MARBLE MADNESS

ELECTIVE ADVENTURE

Complete requirements 1–4. Requirement 5 is optional.

1. Discuss with your family or den the history of marbles, such as where and when the game began. Talk about the different sizes of marbles and what they are made of and used for.

2. Learn about three different marble games, and learn to play one of them. Learn how to keep score. Learn and follow the rules of the game. Play the game with your family, friends, or your den.

3. Learn four words that are used when talking about marbles. Tell what each of the words means and how it relates to playing marbles. Share this information with your den.

4. Complete one of the following:

   A. With your den or family, make a marble obstacle course or marble golf course. Share what you create. Invite everyone to go through your course.

   B. Create your own game using marbles, and design rules for playing the game. Share the game you created with your den, family, or friends. Explain the rules and how to play the game.

   C. With your den or family, create a marble race track. Have at least two lanes so you can race your favorite marbles against each other.

   D. Make a marble maze.

5. With the help of an adult, make a marble bag to hold marbles.

SNAPSHOT OF ADVENTURE

Long before there were board games and video games, kids played with marbles. Those little balls of glass are just as fun to play with now as they were back then. In this adventure, you'll get to play several different marble games, including one you make up yourself. You'll also learn some special words only marble players know and discover how to use marbles in mazes, obstacle courses, and more. Are you ready? Then grab your taws, aggies, and cat's eyes, and let's play marbles!

REQUIREMENT 1 | Discuss with your family or den the history of marbles, such as where and when the game began. Talk about the different sizes of marbles and what they are made of and used for.

Marbles have been around for a long time. Your grandparents probably played marbles, and so did their grandparents. No one knows for sure where and when people started playing marbles, but marbles have been found in Egyptian tombs and in pueblo ruins in the southwestern United States. Early marbles were stones, nuts, fruit pits, and other smooth, round objects.

Here are some fun facts about marbles:

♦ When he was young, the Roman emperor Augustus played with marbles made of nuts.

♦ In 1503, the town of Nuremberg, Germany, passed a law that marbles had to be played outside the town limits.

♦ In the 1700s, people played using chips of marble, which is where the game got its name.

♦ In the early 1900s, marbles were made by machine for the first time.

♦ The British and World Marbles Championship has been played in Tinsley Green, England, every year since 1932, but the tradition began there in 1588.

Marbles come in many different sizes and colors, and they are used for different things. Larger marbles are used as shooters, while smaller marbles are used as targets.

Here are some types of marbles:

- ◆ Cat's eye marbles have a swirl of color inside.
- ◆ Taw marbles are between one-half inch and three-fourths of an inch in diameter, and are used as targets.
- ◆ Alley marbles are made of alabaster or marble. Some are made of glass to look like alabaster or marble.
- ◆ Aggie marbles are made of the mineral agate. Some are made of glass to look like agate. True aggies are good shooters because they are harder than other marbles.
- ◆ Commie or common marbles were originally made out of clay. They are the plainest looking marbles.

Date	**Den Leader's OK**

There are many different games of marbles, and each game has its own set of rules and directions. Here are three games to try.

RINGER

Any number of players can play this game.

- ◆ Draw a ring on the ground about 10 feet across.

- ◆ Put 13 marbles in the middle of the ring arranged in an X shape. They should be about 3 inches apart.

- ◆ The first player kneels outside the ring and uses his or her shooter to try to shoot a marble out of the ring. If it misses, the player's turn is over and he or she picks up the shooter. If the shooter hits and stays in the ring, the player can shoot again from where the shooter stopped. If the shot hits and the shooter goes out of the ring, the player's turn is over. He or she keeps any marbles that go out of the ring.

- ◆ When the first player's turn is over, the second player takes a turn, etc.

- ◆ Keep playing until time is up or most of the marbles have been knocked out. The player with the most marbles is the winner.

PLUMS

This game is for a small number of players.

- Draw two parallel lines about 6 feet apart.

- Each player puts the same number of marbles (called "plums" in this game) on one line a few inches apart. The players stand behind the second line.

- Players take turns shooting at the plums from behind the second line. They keep any plums they knock off the line.

- Keep playing until time is up, if a time limit has been set, or until all the plums have been picked. The player with the most marbles is the winner.

DROPSIES

This game is good for two, three, or four players.

- Draw a square on the ground about 2 feet long by 2 feet wide.

- Each player places five marbles inside the square.

- The first player stands on one side of the square with his or her feet outside the line. That player drops a shooter from above waist height onto one of the other players' marbles to try to knock it out of the square. If that happens and the shooter stays in the square, the player keeps the marble that rolled out, and he or she gets another turn. If a marble is knocked out but the shooter also rolls out, the player keeps the marble that rolled out and his or her turn ends.

- Keep playing until time is up or most of the marbles have been knocked out. The player with the most marbles is the winner.

A Scout is friendly. Everyone will have more fun when you play by the rules and keep the game friendly.

REQUIREMENT 3 | Learn four words that are used when talking about marbles. Tell what each of the words means and how it relates to playing marbles. Share this information with your den.

Like many games and sports, the game of marbles uses some special words. You have already learned some of them, like shooter and alley marbles.

Here are some more:

- Bombies is when you drop your marble onto another marble.

- Dubs is when you knock two or more marbles out of the ring with one shot.

- Keepsies is when you get to keep the marbles you win in a game. Don't play for "keepsies" if you don't want to lose your marbles!

- Friendlies is when you give back the marbles you've won at the end of a game.

- Knuckle down is when you put one knuckle of your shooting hand on the ground as you shoot.

- Histing is when you lift your knuckle as you shoot.

What marbles words do you and your friends use?

3

Date   Den Leader's OK

COMPLETE ONE OF THE FOLLOWING:

REQUIREMENT 4A | With your den or family, make a marble obstacle course or marble golf course. Share what you create. Invite everyone to go through your course.

Shooting marbles around or between objects helps make the game more challenging. Below are two ways you can set up a course to do this. Can you think of another way?

MARBLE OBSTACLE COURSE

Gather some objects from around your house like blocks, paper-towel tubes, yardsticks, and pillows. Use them to form an obstacle course for you and your friend to shoot marbles through.

For extra fun, have your course go down steps or over obstacles. See who can be the first to reach the end of the course.

MARBLE GOLF COURSE

Marble golf is like regular golf. Shoot from one hole to another, counting the number of shots it takes. The object is to get to the last hole with the lowest number of shots. Try to improve your score each time you play.

For an outdoor marble golf course, make indentations in the dirt for your holes. For an indoor marble golf course, use pieces of paper on the floor as holes. A marble is "in" the hole if it stops on the paper.

4A

_____   _____
Date   Den Leader's OK

Some of the best games are the ones you make up yourself. Think up a brand-new game that uses marbles. Decide what the rules are and what the object of the game is. Test it out with one or two friends to make sure it works the way you want it to. If it doesn't, change your game until you are happy with it.

Once your game is ready, teach it to the other members of your den. Who knows? You might invent the next great marbles game!

4B

_____   _____
Date   Den Leader's OK

See whose marbles are the fastest by creating a marble race track. You can make the lanes out of many materials, including felt board, cardboard, PVC pipe, or swimming noodles cut down the middle. For lane separators, use straws or small dowels. Don't forget to mark the start and finish lines.

4C   **Date**   **Den Leader's OK**

A maze is a game where you try to get from start to finish by navigating around a series of twists and turns. The more corners and dead ends the maze has, the more challenging it will be.

Start with a flat surface. A box top works well because the lip around the edge will keep your marble from rolling away. Sketch your maze on the surface, and then glue straws or other dividers on the lines you've drawn. Once the glue has dried, you'll be ready to challenge the maze. How fast can you get through it?

4D

Date	Den Leader's OK

While this requirement is optional, it helps to have a good container to keep track of your marbles.

To make a drawstring bag to hold your marbles, you will need:

♦ A piece of fabric about 5 inches by 9 inches

♦ Needle and thread, for sewing by hand, or a sewing machine (and an adult to help operate it)

♦ A safety pin

♦ A shoestring or piece of cord about 3 feet long

♦ Scissors

PROCEDURE

Fold the long ends of the cloth over about 1 inch, and make a crease. Sew along the cut edges of the fabric to form two pockets.

Fold the fabric in half so the printed side is on the inside. Sew along both edges—but not over the pockets you formed in step 1.

Attach the safety pin to one end of the shoestring or cord. Put the safety pin in the end of one of the pockets, and push it through to the other end.

Next, put the pin in the closest end of the other pocket, and push it through to the other end. Remove the safety pin, and tie the ends of the shoestring or cord in an overhand knot.

Turn the bag right side out. Fill the bag with marbles. To close it, scrunch the fabric at the top together, and tie another overhand knot where the shoestring or cord comes out.

Date

Den Leader's OK

ELECTIVE ADVENTURE

Complete at least four of the following:

1. Think about what makes you laugh. Write down three things that make you laugh.

2. Practice reading tongue twisters.

3. Create your own short story. Remove some nouns, verbs, adjectives, and adverbs from the story, leaving blanks. Without telling the story, have a friend insert his or her own nouns, verbs, adjectives, and adverbs in the story you created.

4. With a partner, play a game that makes you laugh.

5. Share at least two jokes with members of your den to make them laugh.

6. Practice at least two run-ons with your den, and perform them at a pack meeting or campfire program.

SNAPSHOT OF ADVENTURE

Do you like to laugh? Of course you do! Laughing makes you feel good, and it spreads faster than a cold. With just a smile, you can meet a new friend, make someone else smile, and create a happy feeling in yourself and other people. In this adventure, you'll find lots of ways to smile and laugh.

COMPLETE AT LEAST FOUR OF THE FOLLOWING:

REQUIREMENT 1 | Think about what makes you laugh. Write down three things that make you laugh.

Everybody likes to laugh, but not everybody laughs at the same things. Think about what makes you laugh, and make some notes.

THINGS THAT MAKE ME LAUGH

_____

_____

_____

Did you know that laughing actually helps your body? It relaxes your muscles and makes your body and mind feel peaceful and calm. It helps your body fight off germs that could make you sick. It even improves blood  flow in your blood vessels, which helps keep your heart functioning well. So laughter is just what the doctor ordered!

1

Date   **Den Leader's OK**

Tongue twisters are silly statements that trick your tongue. Some are easy to read, and others are really tricky—especially when you say them fast or repeat them. Tongue twisters can give you the giggles when the words that come out of your mouth are not exactly what you were trying to say.

Here are some examples of tongue twisters.

- A big black bug bit a big black bear. But where is the big black bear that the big black bug bit?

- How many yaks could a yak pack pack if a yak pack could pack yaks?

- How much wood could a woodchuck chuck if a woodchuck could chuck wood?

- How many cans can a canner can if a canner can can cans?

- Peter Piper picked a peck of pickled peppers. A peck of pickled peppers Peter Piper picked. If Peter Piper picked a peck of pickled peppers, How many pickled peppers did Peter Piper pick?

- She sells seashells by the seashore.

What other tongue twisters do you know that you could share with your fellow Bear Scouts?

2

_____   _____
Date   **Den Leader's OK**

A silly short story is one where you have replaced some of the words with words that don't fit—or maybe they do! Here's how to create a silly short story.

First, write your own short story. This could be a story about something that happened to you or a letter you might write to a friend or relative. Next, go through your story and take out some of the nouns, verbs, adjectives, and adverbs.

Finally, ask a friend to give you some silly nouns, verbs, adjectives, and adverbs to go in the blanks—but without letting him or her read the story. Write those words in the blanks, then read your story aloud so you can both enjoy it!

SILLY SHORT STORY EXAMPLE

ORIGINAL STORY

What I Did at Cub Scout Camp

This year at Cub Scout camp, I hiked all the way around the lake with my den. During the hike, we saw some deer, a frog, and a lot of butterflies. We also ate trail mix and beef sticks. It was a fun and tiring day.

STORY WITH BLANKS

What I Did at (Event) _____

This year at _____ camp, I _____
            (type of person)   (action verb)

all the way around the _____ with my
                           (noun)

_____ . During the _____ , we saw
(group of people)   (activity)

some _____ , a _____ , and a lot
        (animals)   (animal)

of _____ . We also ate _____ and
      (animals)   (noun)

_____ . It was a _____ and
   (noun)   (adjective)

_____ day.
   (adjective)

STORY WITH BLANKS FILLED IN

What I Did at the Super Bowl

This year at _helicopter pilot_ camp, I _tiptoed_ all the way
around the _Empire State Building_ with my _kazoo orchestra_.
During the _fire drill_, we saw some _wolf spiders_, a
hippopotamus, and a lot of _T. rexes_. We also ate _marbles_
and _remote controls_. It was a _round_ and _sparkly_ day.

3

_____   _____
Date   Den Leader's OK

All games are fun, but some of them make you laugh out loud! Play a game with a friend that makes you laugh.

Having a sense of humor and being able to laugh at yourself can help you become more creative while keeping you healthy. Sharing laughter with your friends and family will help bring you closer together and build stronger relationships.

A Scout is cheerful. So go ahead—let your silly side show, and laugh a little!

Here's a game that you could try:

Pair up with another Bear Scout and sit face to face. Now, try to make each other laugh. You can make faces or sounds, but no touching is allowed. The last person to laugh wins.

After you play, think about these questions: How hard was it to make your buddy laugh? How hard was it for your buddy to make you laugh? What was the final thing that made each of you let out a giggle?

4

_____ _____
Date   Den Leader's OK

Everybody knows at least a few jokes. You can find lots of jokes in *Boys' Life* magazine or in joke books at the library or a bookstore. You can even make up your own.

Here are some examples.

Q: What do you call a Cub Scout who carries another Cub Scout on their back?

A: A taxi Cub!

Q: How does a taxi Cub move?

A: Low-Cub motion!

Q: How did the Cub Scout look after forgetting to take a jacket on the mountain hike?

A: Blue and cold! (blue and gold)

Q: What did the Cub Scout bake as den treats?

A: Cub-cakes!

Q: What did the Cub Scout neckerchief say to the Cub Scout hat?

A: You go on ahead; I'll hang around here.

Q: Why did the rubber chicken cross the road?

A: She wanted to stretch her legs.

Q: Why did the horse cross the road?

A: To reach his *neigh*borhood.

You'll need a partner to ask the questions for knock-knock jokes.

You: Knock knock.
Your Partner: Who's there?
You: Cows go.
Your Partner: Cows go who?
You: No, silly. Cows go MOOO!

You: Knock knock.
Your Partner: Who's there?
You: Interrupting Cow.
Your Partner: Interrupting C…
You: MOO!

You: Knock knock.
Your Partner: Who's there?
You: Who.
Your Partner: Who who?
You: Is there an owl in here?

You: Knock knock.
Your Partner: Who's there?
You: Woo.
Your Partner: Woo, who?
You: Don't get so excited, it's just a joke.

You: Knock knock.

Your Partner: Who's there?

You: Yodalayhi

Your Partner: Yodalayhi who?

You: Hey, why are you yodeling?

You: Knock knock.

Your Partner: Who's there?

You: Cargo

Your Partner: Cargo who?

You: Cargo vroom vroom.

HOW TO BE FUNNY

How can you be funny when you tell jokes? First, start with funny jokes! If you don't find a joke funny, how can you expect your friends to find it funny? Next, think about who you will be telling it to. A younger brother or sister might not understand a joke about math class, for example. Finally, practice the joke, including any facial expressions, body movements, or hand gestures that will help make it funnier. And remember: practice makes perfect!

5

_____   _____
Date   Den Leader's OK

Run-ons are quick gags that are used during downtime at a campfire program or pack meeting. They can involve one person or many. When performing your run-on, remember to speak loudly and clearly so the audience can hear what you are saying.

Here are some examples:

Scout 1: Runs out screaming, "They're on me! They're on me!"

Scout 2: "What's on you?"

Scout 1: "My clothes."

Scout 1: Runs out screaming, "They're after me! They're after me!"

Scout 2: "Who's after you?"

Scout 1: "The squirrels. They think I'm nuts."

Scout 1: Walks out dragging a rope across the ground

Scout 2: "Why are you dragging that rope?"

Scout 1: "Have you ever tried pushing one?"

6

Date   **Den Leader's OK**

ROBOTICS

ELECTIVE ADVENTURE

Complete at least four of the following:

1. Identify six tasks performed by robots.

2. Learn about some instances where a robot could be used in place of a human for work. Research one robot that does this type of work, and present what you learn to your den.

3. Build a robot hand. Show how it works like a human hand and how it is different from a human hand.

4. Build your own robot.

5. Visit a place that uses robots.

SNAPSHOT OF ADVENTURE

When we think of robots, we almost always think of human-like figures that have arms and legs and talk in funny voices. But robots come in many shapes and sizes, from one-armed machines that look like construction cranes to roving navigators that can travel over rocks and sand.

So what exactly is a robot? It's a machine that operates automatically and does jobs humans don't want to do or can't do. In this adventure, you will learn about robots and, even better, you'll get to build your own. Your robot will be simple, but maybe someday you will build a robot to clean up your bedroom!

COMPLETE AT LEAST FOUR OF THE FOLLOWING:

REQUIREMENT 1 | Identify six tasks performed by robots.

What comes to mind when you think about robots? What robots have you seen on TV or in movies? Do you have a robotic toy at home, or does your parent work with robots on the job? Does someone you know have a robot to help with chores around the home? Working with your den leader or another adult, learn more about real robots.

On a separate paper, list at least six tasks of robots.

1 _____   _____
   Date   **Den Leader's OK**

Do you remember how we said that a robot is a machine that does jobs so humans don't have to? Those jobs usually fall into four categories: dangerous, dirty, dull, and difficult.

DANGEROUS

Robots often do jobs that are too dangerous for humans to perform. Robots can also go places humans can't, like the bottom of the ocean or the surface of another planet. Law enforcement officers use robots to detonate or defuse bombs. NASA has sent several robots, called rovers, to Mars to study the planet's climate and geology.

DIRTY

There are also places humans can go but would rather avoid. For example, robots are used to inspect sewer pipes and storage

tanks for cracks or clogs. That's a stinky, dirty job for a human; but for a robot, it's all in a day's work.

DULL

Imagine spending your entire day screwing lids onto juice bottles. Robots are excellent at doing boring jobs quickly and easily. They can cap bottles, glaze doughnuts, paint cars, and even pick things up and move them around. You might even have a robot at home that vacuums the floors!

DIFFICULT

Robots can also do tasks that humans find too complex or difficult. Some robots have the power to lift huge amounts of materials and transport them where they are needed. Other robots help doctors perform delicate surgeries. Some can even travel through your body taking pictures along the way so your doctor can see whether you have any illnesses or diseases.

Choose one of these four categories of tasks. Then, with your parent's or guardian's help, research one specific robot that performs those tasks. Create a visual presentation of what you have learned, and share it with your den at your next meeting.

2

Date   Den Leader's OK

Most robots are very complicated machines, but you can make a simple robot hand with some materials you probably have at home. That's what you will do for this requirement.

Materials and Tools

- Narrow rubber bands
- Drinking straws
- Stiff cardboard
- Tape
- Scissors
- Nylon cord
- Ruler
- Pen

Instructions

1. Cut a piece of cardboard that measures 10 centimeters by 10 centimeters. This will be the palm of the robot hand. Next, cut three pieces of cardboard that measure 2 centimeters by 9 centimeters each. These will be the fingers.

2. Cut one of the fingers into three equal pieces 2 centimeters by 3 centimeters.

three equal pieces

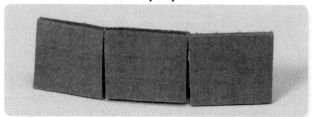

3. Put the pieces back together and reconnect them using tape. Write "inside" on the side of the finger that is facing up. Flip the finger over so the inside is facing down.

tape on inside

inside

4. Cut a piece of rubber band 5 centimeters long. Lay it across the first joint, and tape it down on both sides of the joint. Fold the ends of the rubber band over the tape, and tape them down; this will keep the rubber band from pulling loose.

tape   **5-centimeter-long rubber band**

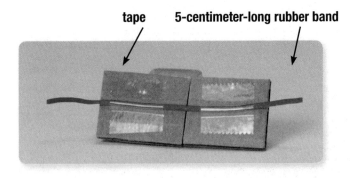

tape firmly over the bent rubber band

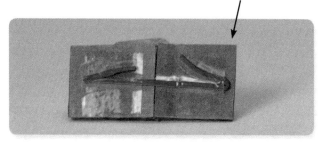

5. Repeat step 4 to make the second joint.

connecting fingers to hand

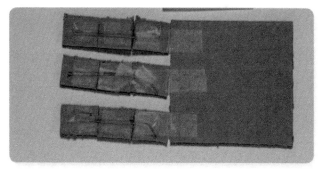

6. Turn the hand over, and tape the finger to the palm. Then, turn the hand back over so the inside is facing down.

7. Cut a piece of rubber band 5 centimeters long. Lay it across the joint between the finger and the palm. Tape the rubber band down as you did in step 4. Turn the hand back over so the inside is facing up.

8. Cut a piece of nylon cord 35 centimeters long, and cut four pieces of straw 2 centimeters long. Tape one end of the cord to the tip of the finger. Thread the straw pieces onto the cord, and tape one to the middle of each section of the finger. Tape the last one to the palm.

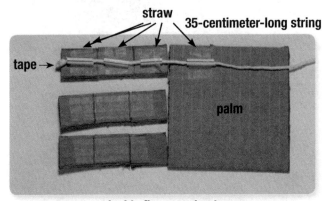

inside finger and palm

9. Repeat steps 2 through 8 to make the other two fingers. You now have a complete robot hand!

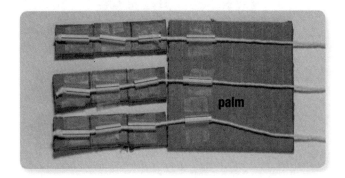

Did you notice how these instructions use the metric system? Scientists always use the metric system in their work. It may be different from what you're used to, but it is really easy to understand.

With your robot hand, try to pick up empty water bottles and other lightweight objects. Just hold the robot hand's palm with one of your own hands, and pull the cords with your other hand.

Talk with your parent or den leader about how your robot hand is similar to a real hand and how it is different. One big difference you may notice is that your robot hand doesn't have a thumb. Why do you think having a thumb is important? How could you add a thumb to your robot hand?

3

_____   _____
Date   **Den Leader's OK**

With help from your den leader, parent, or another adult, build a robot. You can buy a robot kit or use ordinary household items to create your own.

What is the purpose of your robot? Does it handle one of the jobs you learned about in requirement 3? How well does it do its job? What improvements could you make?

Remember to think about safety before you start building and while you are working. Wear safety glasses while you are building your robot, and ask an adult to help you with tools. Always disconnect the batteries or unplug the power cord while you are working on your robot and after you are done using it.

4 _____   _____
        Date   **Den Leader's OK**

Robots don't just exist in science fiction movies. They exist down the street. With the help of your parent or den leader, find a company, school, or organization that uses robots, and make a visit. Find out how and why the robots are used. If possible, watch the robots in action, and talk with the people who operate them.

_____   _____
Date   **Den Leader's OK**

Robots can be really fun to build! You get to work with your hands and your brain at the same time. When you get to middle school or high school, they may have a robotics team you could join.

SALMON RUN

ELECTIVE ADVENTURE

Complete requirements 1–4 plus two others.

1. Explain the importance of response personnel or lifeguards in a swimming area. Tell how the buddy system works and why it is important.

2. Visit a local pool or swimming area with your den or family. Go swimming or take a swimming lesson.

3. Explain the safety rules that you need to follow before participating in boating.

4. Identify the safety equipment needed when going boating.

5. Demonstrate correct rowing or paddling form. Explain how rowing and canoeing are good exercise.

6. Show how to do both a reach rescue and a throw rescue.

7. Demonstrate the front crawl swim stroke to your den or family.

8. Name the three swimming ability groups for the Boy Scouts of America.

9. Earn the BSA beginner swim classification.

SNAPSHOT OF ADVENTURE

Did you know that nearly three-fourths of the earth is covered by water? It is! If you want to explore a lot of the world, you have to go by boat or know how to swim.

Grizzly bears are animals that know how to swim even though they live in the forest. They swim in ice-cold rivers to catch the salmon they eat. As a Bear Scout, you will get to go swimming, too—not to catch fish but to have fun. In this adventure, you'll learn about swimming and boating and how to stay safe around the water.

COMPLETE REQUIREMENTS 1-4 PLUS TWO OTHERS.

REQUIREMENT 1 | **Explain the importance of response personnel or lifeguards in a swimming area. Tell how the buddy system works and why it is important.**

When you go swimming, three people can help you stay safe. The first is you! You stay safe when you follow the rules of the lake or pool. Stay in the designated swimming area, don't run or engage in horseplay, and don't dive in shallow water.

The second person who can help you stay safe is your buddy—and you can do the same for him or her. Always have your buddy with you when you enter and leave the swimming area, and always swim near your buddy. When someone calls "Buddy check," you and your buddy should grab each other's hands and hold them high.

The third person who can help you stay safe is the lifeguard. Lifeguards are specially trained to help swimmers who get into trouble. They constantly watch the swimming area, looking for swimmers who need help. They know how to rescue swimmers who are in trouble without putting themselves in danger.

Date **Den Leader's OK**

REQUIREMENT 2 | Visit a local pool or swimming area with your den or family. Go swimming or take a swimming lesson.

Whether you live in the city or the country, there is probably a place nearby where you can go swimming. There may even be an indoor pool that is open year-round. For this requirement, visit a pool or swimming area with your den or family. Follow the rules below to help keep you and your den or family safe.

BASIC RULES OF SAFE SWIMMING

1. Be physically fit.
2. Have a qualified adult present whenever you swim.
3. Swim in areas that have already been checked and have no deep holes, stumps, rocks, cans, or glass.
4. If you can't swim, don't go in water more than chest deep.
5. If you can swim 50 feet, it's safe to go in water up to the top of your head. Go in deep water only if you are a good swimmer.
6. Swim with a buddy. That way, you can help each other if one of you gets into trouble.
7. Obey the rules.

Have a good time in the water, and learn to swim a little better each time you go in.

A Scout is obedient. Listen to the adults in charge so you know the rules at the swimming area you are visiting.

_____   _____
Date   Den Leader's OK

REQUIREMENT 3 | Explain the safety rules that you need to follow before participating in boating.

Boating is a fun way to explore a lake or get to your favorite fishing spot. However, before you leave shore, be sure you know—and follow—these safety rules:

* Always wear a life jacket when you go boating. Be sure the life jacket fits well and is snuggly buckled.

* Check the weather before departing. If it looks bad, keep your boat at the dock. You don't want to be in the middle of a lake during a lightning storm!

* Keep the boat balanced and weight spread evenly. This will help keep the boat from tipping over.

* Don't overload the boat. Too much weight could sink it.

* Stay low and in the center of the boat. Step into the center of the boat when you get in or change seats. Don't stand up in the boat; crouch down instead.

* If the boat tips over, hang on to it until help comes. Even a boat that is full of water can still float.

* Keep a lookout for swimmers and other boaters. Be careful not to get too close to other people on or in the water.

* Always have a buddy. When you are boating or swimming, use the buddy system. Watch out for your buddy, and your buddy will watch out for you.

* Only go boating with adult supervision. The Boy Scouts of America has Safety Afloat rules that adult leaders follow to keep you safe.

3

_____   _____
Date   Den Leader's OK

No matter what kind of boating you do, you will need to have a properly fitted life jacket. The best kind is a Type III life jacket that has been approved by the U.S. Coast Guard.

To make sure your life jacket fits, do this:
- Check the label to see if it is designed for your size and weight.
- Put the jacket on, buckle it, and tighten the straps.
- Hold your arms over your head. Have a friend pull up on the tops of the arm openings. If the the jacket rides up over your chin or face, it is too loose.

It is always a good idea to take the Cub Scout Six Essentials when boating.

CUB SCOUT SIX ESSENTIALS

☐ First-aid kit

☐ Flashlight
(check the batteries)

☐ Trail food

☐ Filled water bottle

☐ Sun protection

☐ Emergency whistle

Date

Den Leader's OK

Rowing and canoeing are good exercise. They help build strong muscles, and they provide good aerobic exercise because they make your heart and lungs work harder.

If you have never been rowing or canoeing before, you will need to learn and practice the strokes that make the boat go.

ROWING STROKES

When you row, you actually face the back of the boat. (Your buddy can help you steer.) Hold the oar handles firmly with your knuckles up and wrists and arms straight. Bend forward a little bit.

Each stroke has four parts:

♦ Catch. Lower the oar blades edgewise into the water behind you, not too deep.

Catch

+ Pull. Lean backward, pulling on the oars and bending your arms until your elbows come in against your ribs.

Pull

+ Feather. Lift the oars slightly out of the water, and turn your knuckles up toward your face so the blades are flat above the water's surface.

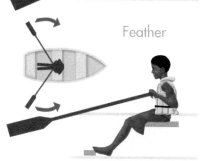

Feather

+ Recover. Bend forward and straighten your wrists and arms, ready to begin another stroke.

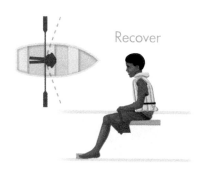

Recover

To do the backstroke, push on the oars instead of pulling. To turn, pull on one oar while you push on the other.

CANOEING STROKES

With canoeing, both people in the canoe paddle, usually on opposite sides and stroking at the same time. The person in the back steers and gives direction. The person in the front adds power and helps the canoe go straight.

To stroke a paddle properly, hold it firmly with both hands—one hand on the top of the handle and the other hand just above the throat, the area where the paddle starts to get wide. Bend forward a little, and let your upper body rotate as you paddle.

The forward stroke has four parts:

♦ Catch. Lower the paddle blade edgewise into the water in front of you, not too deep.

Catch

♦ Power. Pull backward to your hip, keeping the paddle straight up and down.

Power

- Feather. Lift the paddle slightly out of the water, with the blade flat above the water's surface.

Feather and Recover

- Recover. Rotate the paddle forward and straighten your wrists and arms, ready to begin another stroke.

- Sweep. To do the backstroke, push on the paddle instead of pulling. Use sweeps to turn a canoe. Reach out with the paddle and move it in a quarter circle, either forward or backward. Or use draw and pry strokes, pulling or pushing the paddle straight toward or away from the canoe.

Sweep

Now it's your chance to demonstrate these steps. You can practice before you get into a boat by standing in knee high water and paddling like you would if you were in a canoe. Using a real oar or paddle, show your den leader the correct form for rowing or paddling. Explain why rowing and canoeing are good exercise. When you're ready to head out in a real boat, you'll know what to do!

5

_____   _____
Date   Den Leader's OK

Whenever you go swimming, a lifeguard should be on duty to help. He or she will help any swimmers who get into trouble.

What if someone needs help and no lifeguard is around? As a Bear Scout, you are not expected to do the rescue work of a trained adult. However, there are some things you can do.

First, send a friend to call for help. Next, if no adult is there, try to help from shore. If the person is close to shore, lie down and reach with your hand. Otherwise, use whatever is available, like a towel, a tree branch, a fishing pole, or a canoe paddle. Be careful not to let the person pull you into the water. If possible, anchor yourself to another person or to a solid object like the edge of a dock.

You can practice reach rescues in the shallow end of a swimming pool. If you are inside, you can pretend that a rug on the floor is the water.

A Scout is brave. Learning safe ways to rescue someone can help you feel brave in an emergency.

If you can't reach the person, you can throw a rope, a life ring, or anything that will float. The object will give the person support. If it is tied to a rope, you can pull the person to shore.

To practice throw rescues, you can create your own throw line at home. Just attach a rope to a plastic milk jug with a little water in it. Go outside and have a friend stand about 20 feet from you. Practice throwing the jug to your friend—but don't hit him or her with it!

6

_____
Date

_____
Den Leader's OK

The front crawl is one of many strokes that you will learn in swimming. It is one of the best strokes to use when you take the swim test. A good way to learn the front crawl is to practice with your legs first and then with your arms.

Your legs will do a flutter kick. You do this by moving your legs up and down in the water, pressing down on the water with the top of your foot. Practice the flutter kick by holding onto a kickboard or the side of the pool.

Next, practice with your arms. Float on your stomach, and practice reaching out as far as you can in front of you, one arm at a time. Cup each hand, and scoop water down and back toward your body as your arm goes around in a circle.

Now, try using your arms and legs at the same time. Relax, and don't hurry. As you get better, you will be able to swim farther with less effort.

7

Date   **Den Leader's OK**

Swimmer

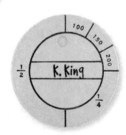

Before you go swimming or boating at a Scouting activity, you must demonstrate your swimming ability. Depending on how well you can swim, you will be classified as a nonswimmer, a beginner, or a swimmer. That classification allows you into different swimming areas.

Don't worry if you can't do all the swimmer requirements. Instead, make it your goal to become a swimmer! You can improve your swimming ability by asking an adult for help and by practicing. As you get better, you can ask to retake the swim test at another time.

Beginner

Nonswimmer

8

Date   Den Leader's OK

REQUIREMENT 9 | Earn the BSA beginner swim classification.

To be classified as a beginner, you must:

• Jump feetfirst into water over your head in depth.

• Level off, and swim 25 feet on the surface.

• Stop, turn sharply, and resume swimming.

Try that test under the supervision of a lifeguard. If you pass it, you'll be well on your way to swimming like a bear!

9

Date   Den Leader's OK

SUPER SCIENCE

ELECTIVE ADVENTURE

Complete at least four of the following:

1. Make static electricity by rubbing a balloon or a plastic or rubber comb against another material, such as a fleece blanket or wool sweater. Explain what you learned.

2. Conduct one other static electricity investigation. Explain what you learned.

3. Do a sink-or-float investigation. Explain what you learned.

4. Do a color-morphing investigation. Explain what you learned.

5. Do a color-layering investigation. Explain what you learned.

SNAPSHOT OF ADVENTURE

Have you ever wondered why the sky is blue or how gravity works or what makes a rainbow? Scientists wonder about those things, too. Then, they figure out the answers using experiments. Some of those experiments are really fun because they use stuff that is gooey, oozy, splishy, and splashy—just the kind of stuff Bear Scouts enjoy! In this adventure, you'll get to do some science projects that are a little bit messy and really amazing. So put on your lab coat, and get ready to do some super science!

ANSWERING SCIENTIFIC QUESTIONS

Scientists try to create a fair test when they want to answer a question. The steps below can help you answer questions like a scientist:

1. Ask a question. (What do you want to discover?)

2. Do research. (What have other scientists already learned?)

3. Make a good guess at the answer. (This guess is called a hypothesis.)

4. Test your hypothesis with an experiment. (This is the fun part!)

5. Decide whether your hypothesis was supported by the information you collected.

6. Share what you discovered.

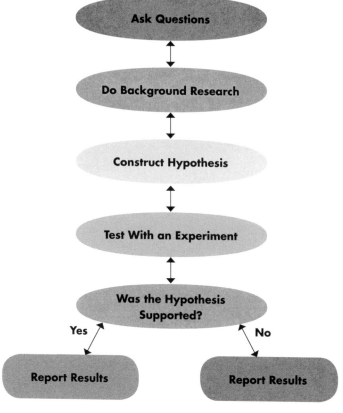

REQUIREMENT 1 | Make static electricity by rubbing a balloon or a plastic or rubber comb against another material, such as a fleece blanket or wool sweater. Explain what you learned.

You may have walked across a carpeted floor to pet your dog and gotten a shock. You may have taken off your winter hat and found that your hair was standing straight up in the air. Those things happen because of static electricity.

To understand static electricity, you have to understand atoms. Everything around us is made up of very small things called atoms. Those atoms are made up of even smaller things, including protons and electrons. Protons have a positive charge, and electrons have a negative charge. Each atom usually has the same number of protons and electrons, but if two atoms bump into each other, electrons from one atom can get rubbed off onto the other atom.

As you walk across a carpeted floor (especially if you drag your feet), extra electrons build up on your body. When you touch your dog, those electrons jump onto the dog, causing a little spark of static electricity.

Why does your hair stand up when you pull off your winter hat? That happens because all your individual hairs now have a positive charge and are repelling each other. (This is like trying to hold the positive sides of two magnets together.)

Static electricity also makes some things stick together, such as hiking socks and dryer sheets. For this requirement, try to make objects stick to an electrically charged balloon or comb. Blow up a balloon or take a comb and rub each of them separately against a fleece blanket or wool sweater. Then see what objects will stick to the balloon or comb. Discuss your findings with your den.

TESTING STATIC ELECTRICITY

Which of these objects will stick to a balloon or comb? Write down your prediction and then write down what actually happened.

Object	Prediction	Result of investigation
Tissue paper		
Aluminum foil		
Cardboard scrap		
Paper scrap		
Yarn or string		
Pom-pom		
Chenille stem		
Ribbon		
Cloth		
Foam		
Coin		

1 _____   _____
         Date   Den Leader's OK

For this requirement, fill a dry, empty plastic bottle with small foam beads (like the kind in beanbag chairs). Stand in front of a mirror, and rub the bottle on your head. What happens to the beads?

Now, touch your other hand to the bottle. Do the beads move toward your hand or away from it? Experiment with other objects to check the reaction of the foam beads.

Date

Den Leader's OK

Have you ever wondered if an egg will sink or float? Do you think adding anything to the water would change the outcome? Let's find out!

Materials

- Three large cups, about 12 ounces, all the same size
- Three fresh eggs
- 2 tablespoons of salt
- 2 tablespoons of sugar
- Water
- A spoon

Instructions

1. Fill all three cups half full with water.
2. Stir the salt into the first cup and the sugar into the second cup.
3. Leave the third cup alone.
4. In the chart on the next page, write down what you think will happen when you add an egg to each cup.
5. Add an egg to each cup. Observe what happens to each egg, and write down the results.

SINK OR FLOAT

Will salt or sugar affect whether an egg floats? Write down your prediction, and then write down what actually happened.

Cup	Prediction	Result of experiment
Cup 1 — Salt added		
Cup 2 — Sugar added		
Cup 3 — Nothing added		

How did your predictions compare to what you observed? Why do you think the eggs did different things?

This investigation shows how scientists use variables. A variable is something that changes. By changing just one variable at a time, you proved how sugar and salt affect how eggs float. The plain water is called the control because it doesn't change. Since the control is the same in each cup, we can use it to compare the results with the salt and the sugar.

3

Date

Den Leader's OK

You may have heard that oil and water do not mix. In fact, they will actually push away from each other if they are in the same space! To investigate this principle, you will mix some food coloring into oil.

Materials

- A large jar or clear vase
- Water to fill the jar halfway
- A measuring cup
- A spoon
- 2 tablespoons of cooking oil
- 3 drops each of red, blue, and yellow liquid food coloring

Instructions

1. Fill the jar or vase halfway with water.

2. In the measuring cup, mix the oil and the food coloring together.

3. Pour this mixture slowly into the water, and watch what happens.

What is happening? Since food coloring is water-based, it will separate from the oil and float through the water in amazing color morphs. If you have time, try different color combinations.

4

_____   _____
Date   Den Leader's OK

For this requirement, you will create a rainbow in a cup using sugar, water, and food coloring.

Materials
- 15 tablespoons of sugar
- 15 tablespoons of warm water
- Red, green, blue, and yellow liquid food coloring
- Six clear cups
- A spoon

Instructions

1. Put five cups in a row on the table.

2. Add one tablespoon of sugar to the first cup, two tablespoons to the second cup, three to the third, four to the fourth, and five to the fifth.

3. Add three tablespoons of lukewarm water to each cup. Stir until most of the sugar dissolves.

4. Add a drop or two of food coloring to the first four cups, one color per cup. In the fifth cup, mix two colors.

5. Take the fifth cup (the one with the most sugar) and pour half of its contents into the sixth cup (the one that's empty).

6. Hold the spoon, bowl side up, against the inside of the sixth cup. Slowly and gently pour half the contents of the fourth cup onto the spoon. (Pouring onto the spoon keeps the two liquids from mixing in the cup.) Do the same thing with the third, second, and first cups.

What is happening? Adding sugar to the water causes it to become denser as the sugar molecules take over the space. The more sugar you add, the denser the water becomes. That's why you can "stack" the colored water as long as you pour it gently.

5

Date   Den Leader's OK

A WORLD OF SOUND

ELECTIVE ADVENTURE

Complete all of the following:

1. Make an mbira.
2. Make a sistrum.
3. Make a rain stick.

SNAPSHOT OF ADVENTURE

What do Zimbabwe, Egypt, and Chile have in common? Amazing music! The native peoples of those countries have been making musical instruments for thousands of years. We're not talking guitars, pianos, and trumpets, however. We're talking instruments like the mbira, the sistrum, and the rain stick.

In this adventure, you'll use your imagination to travel to these distant lands and learn how to make your own musical instruments. By the time your journey is over, you'll have enough instruments to start your own band. Ready to go? Our first stop is Zimbabwe, home of the magnificent mbira. Let's get this musical adventure started!

> Before you start using tools to make an instrument, check out the Baloo the Builder adventure. You'll find some important safety tips there.

COMPLETE ALL OF THE FOLLOWING:

REQUIREMENT 1 | Make an mbira.

Welcome to Zimbabwe, a country in southern Africa! People have lived here for thousands and thousands of years, including the Shona people, who make up most of the population. If you go to a party called a mabira in Zimbabwe, you'll probably hear people playing the mbira (pronounced em-BEE-ra), or thumb piano.

Traditional mbiras have 22 to 28 keys made of forged metal. Your mbira will use bobby pins instead, but you'll still get a good idea of what an mbira sounds like.

Materials and Tools

- A board about 6 inches wide and 8 inches long
- Four craft sticks
- Four bobby pins
- Safety glasses
- Brads or wire nails and a hammer
- Adhesive tape
- Wire cutters
- Hot glue gun

Instructions

1. With help from an adult, glue two craft sticks side by side across the middle of the board.

2. While wearing safety glasses, cut each bobby pin in half. Trim the eight pieces you now have so each one is a little shorter than the one before it.

3. Lay the bobby pin pieces on top of the craft sticks from shortest to longest. Align their ends with the craft sticks. At the other end, they will be different lengths.

4. Tape the bobby pin pieces down so they don't move.

5. With help from an adult, glue the last two craft sticks on top of the first two. To make the mbira sturdier, use the hammer to drive brads through the ends of the craft sticks and between each pair of bobby pin pieces.

6. Bend the bobby pin pieces up at about a 45 degree angle from the board. Get ready to play!

How to Play

To play your mbira, just pluck the metal "keys" with your thumbs. Since they are different lengths, they'll make different sounds. See if you can play a simple tune like "Happy Birthday" or "Twinkle, Twinkle, Little Star." How would you describe the sound the mbira makes?

You can also try some investigations with your mbira. Instead of using your thumbs, use a spoon or a craft stick to pluck the keys. Does that make a difference? What if you put the mbira inside a box and play it? Does the sound change?

| Date | Den Leader's OK |

REQUIREMENT 2 | Make a sistrum.

For our next instrument, we will travel 3,000 miles north to Egypt and 3,000 years back in time. Here in ancient Egypt, musicians used an instrument called the sistrum to play songs for the pharaohs (the kings of Egypt). Many wall paintings from royal tombs show sistrums being played.

The original sistrums were made out of bone, wood, and strong plant fibers. We'll use materials that you can find around your home or get at a craft store.

Materials and Tools
- Wire clothes hanger
- Electrical tape
- Two craft sticks
- Some fishing line or thin wire (the kind florists or picture-framers use is great)
- Buttons, jingle bells, metal washers, and other small items that have holes in them
- Wire cutters

Instructions
1. Straighten out the curved part of the clothes hanger (the part that goes over the closet rod). This will form your sistrum's handle.
2. Put the craft sticks on either side of the handle. Tightly wrap electrical tape around the handle and both sticks. Start your wrapping just below the craft sticks and end it just above the

craft sticks so they won't slide up and down. The sticks will make the handle more comfortable to hold.

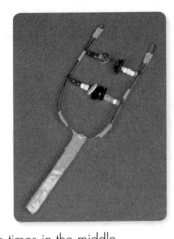

3. With the help of an adult, cut the long side of the clothes hanger in half using the wire cutters. Bend each side down so you have what looks like a big letter Y.

4. On each side of the Y, wrap electrical tape around the pieces to hold them together. Do this at the top and the bottom and two or three times in the middle. Be sure to leave spaces for the next step.

5. Attach a piece of fishing line or thin wire to one side of the Y. String some buttons, bells, washers, or other items on the line or wire. Then tie the other end to the other side of the Y. Do this again in one or two other places, as shown in the picture.

How to Play

It's easy to play the sistrum. Just shake the instrument or flip it from side to side to make the items in the middle swish, jingle, or clang together. Try to match the rhythm in a song. Was it easier to match the beat by shaking the sistrum or by sliding it back and forth?

What sound from nature does your sistrum make? See if you can make it sound like the wind in the reeds (a type of plant that grows in low marshy ground) or like the gentle running water of the Nile River.

2

_____   _____
Date   **Den Leader's OK**

REQUIREMENT 3 | Make a rain stick.

For our last stop, we'll travel to Chile, a long, narrow country on the western side of South America where we learn how to make a rain stick. People in the Diaguita (pronounced DEE-uh-GEE-tuh, where the G sound is like in the word "geese") tribe here have been making rain sticks for many years. Rain sticks have also been made by tribes in Panama, Ecuador, Peru, and other countries in Central and South America.

The original rain sticks were made out of pieces of hollow cactus. People cut the spikes off and drove them into the cactus like nails. These spikes caught seeds and pebbles as they fell from one end to the other, making an amazing rain-like sound.

For your rain stick, you'll use a cardboard mailing tube. A "maze" of wire and chenille stems will take the place of the spikes.

One really fun thing about rain sticks is that each one is different. If you and a friend both make rain sticks, each one will have its own special sound.

Materials and Tools

- Cardboard mailing tube (try to find one with plastic end caps)
- Crayons, markers, and other art supplies
- Paper
- Packaging tape
- Thin wire (the kind florists or picture-framers use is great)
- Four or five chenille stems

- A variety of small objects like uncooked rice, beans, small beads, dry macaroni, small pebbles, and buttons
- Wire cutters

Instructions

1. With the help of an adult, use the wire cutters to cut a piece of wire two or three times as long as the tube. Put tape over the ends so you don't poke yourself. Twist and tangle the wire so it is the same length as the tube and will fit inside.

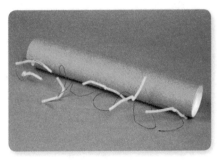

2. Cut the chenille stems in half and twist them around the wire every 6 inches or so like the picture shows. If your mailing tube is extra wide, use whole chenille stems so that they stretch across the tube.

3. Carefully slide the wire inside the tube. Tape each end to the inside of the tube so it won't slide up and down.

4. Put the cap on one end of the tube or tape a piece of paper over the opening.

5. Now comes the fun part. Pour a handful of rice, beans, or other small objects into the tube. Hold your hand over the open end and slowly turn the tube upside down.

6. If you like the sound you hear, put the cap on the other end of the tube or tape paper over the opening. Otherwise, pour the objects into a bowl and try again. You will discover that different objects make different sounds. If you want a quiet rain stick, use birdseed, rice, or small pasta like orzo. For a louder rain stick, use beans, buttons, elbow macaroni, or pebbles.

7. Once you like your rain stick's sound, cap or tape over the open end. If you're using a tube with plastic end caps, put tape over both caps so nothing can spill out.

8. Decorate the outside of the mailing tube with symbols, your name, or anything else you like.

How to Play

You can play your rain stick lots of different ways. Turn it over slowly to make a rain-like sound. Shake it gently to create a beat. Tap on it to make a sound like a drum. See who in your den can make the coolest sound with his or her rain stick! Better yet, you can bring all of your new instruments together and put on a show!

3

_____
Date

_____
Den Leader's OK

The following awards can be earned while you are a Cub Scout. Check with your pack leaders or go online (with a parent's or guardian's permission) to learn more.

Conservation Good Turn Award

The Conservation Good Turn is an award packs may earn by partnering with a conservation or environmental organization to choose and carry out a Good Turn in their home communities.

Outdoor Activity Award

Tiger, Wolf, Bear, and Webelos Scouts have the opportunity to earn the Cub Scout Outdoor Activity Award. Scouts may earn the award in each of the program years as long as the requirements are completed again each year. Cub Scouts complete specific requirements for each rank, including a number of different outdoor activities.

National Summertime Pack Award

The National Summertime Pack Award encourages packs to be active when school is out for the summer. Youth and adult pack members can earn the award by taking part in one activity per month in June, July, and August.

Emergency Preparedness Award

Cub Scouts who want to take steps to prepare themselves and their families in case of an emergency may earn the Emergency Preparedness Award. Cub Scouts may earn the award at each rank for completing increasingly challenging requirements.

STEM/Nova Awards

The Nova awards for Cub Scouts are for Wolf, Bear, and Webelos Scouts who are interested in learning more about science, technology, engineering, and mathematics. These awards may not be earned by Lion or Tiger Scouts.

For their first Nova awards, Scouts have the opportunity to earn the Nova award patch, followed by three more π pin-on devices. The patch and the three devices represent each of the four STEM topics. The Supernova awards have more challenging requirements and recognize more in-depth, advanced achievement in STEM-related activities.

World Conservation Award

The World Conservation Award for Cub Scouts provides an opportunity for individual Wolf, Bear, and Webelos Scouts to "think globally" and "act locally" to preserve and improve our environment. This program is designed to make youth members aware that all nations are closely related through natural resources, and that we are interdependent with our world environment.

Requirements for this award must be completed *in addition to* any similar requirements completed for rank. This award may not be earned by Lion or Tiger Scouts.

Bobcat Trail

Your name _____

Fill in seven tracks to earn the Bobcat badge.

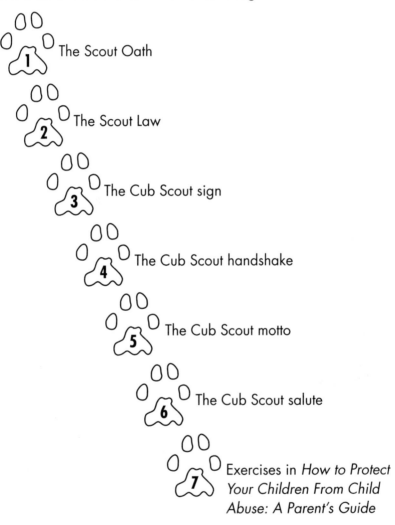

1. The Scout Oath

2. The Scout Law

3. The Cub Scout sign

4. The Cub Scout handshake

5. The Cub Scout motto

6. The Cub Scout salute

7. Exercises in *How to Protect Your Children From Child Abuse: A Parent's Guide*

Bear Adventure Tracking

1. Complete each of the following Bear required adventures with your den or family:

Required Adventures

Youth Protection
Same as Bobcat No. 7

Baloo the Builder
Complete all

Bear Claws
Complete all

Bear Necessities
Do 1, 2, 3, and 4;
5 and 6 are optional

**Fellowship and
Duty to God**
Complete all

Fur, Feathers, and Ferns
Do 1 and THREE others

Paws for Action
Do 1 and TWO others

2. Complete at least one Bear elective adventure of your den or family's choosing.

   My elective adventure: _____

3. With your parent, guardian, or other caring adult, complete the exercises in the pamphlet *How to Protect Your Children From Child Abuse: A Parent's Guide*.

4. Earn the Cyber Chip award for your age.*
   *See full requirements on page 28.

Elective Adventures

A Bear Goes Fishing   1   2   3   4

Bear Picnic Basket   1   2   3   4   5

Beat of the Drum   1   2   3A   3B   3C   4A   4B   4C   4D

Critter Care   1A   1B   2A   2B   3A   3B

Forensics   1   2   3A   3B   4A   4B   4C

Grin and Bear It   1   2   3   4   5

Make It Move   1   2   3   4A   4B

Marble Madness   1   2   3   4A   4B   4C   4D   5

Roaring Laughter   1   2   3   4   5   6

Robotics   1   2   3   4   5

Salmon Run   1 2 3 4 5 6 7 8 9

Super Science   1 2 3 4 5

A World of Sound   1 2 3

GET SET FOR THE WEBELOS ADVENTURES!

So what's next? Well, if you have finished the third grade or are now 10 years old, you can begin to work on the Webelos adventures! Keep on Cub Scouting!

CREDITS

Acknowledgments

The Boy Scouts of America gratefully acknowledges the contributions of the many Cub Scouts, Scouters, subject experts, and staff throughout the nation for their help in preparing the *Bear Handbook*. A special thank-you to the Cub Scout Handbook Task Force for their leadership: national Cub Scout chair, Lucia Cronin; task force committee members Linda Baker, Steve Bowen, Silvia de la Cruz, and Michelle Holmes; and national director, Cub Scouting, Anthony Berger.

Photo/Illustration Credits

Illustration

Jeff Ebbeler—page 200

Rube Goldberg Artwork Copyright © and TM Rube Goldberg Inc. All Rights Reserved. RUBE GOLDBERG® is a registered trademark of Rube Goldberg Inc. All materials used with permission. Rubegoldberg.com—page 209

Aleksey Ivanov—pages 228, 229, and 234–235 (*all*)

John McDearmon—page 9

Rob Schuster—pages 31–37 (*all*), 44 (*all*), 57 (*both*), 69, 98–99 (*all*), 129, 132 (*both*), 204 (*both*), 207–208 (*all*), and 258–261 (*all*)

Photography

Dan Bryant—pages 8 (*both*), 89–91 (*exercises*), 110 (*salute*), 120, 176, 181, 212, 217, 221, 238, 268, 276, and 289

BSA—pages 3, 82, 148 (*pancakes*), 149 (*corn*), 233, and 248

Tom Copeland—pages 28, 31–35, 39, and 47

Phil Davis—page 183

Al Drago—pages 21 (*bottom*), 41, 52, 106, 108, 118, 145 (*top*), 155, and 157

W. Garth Dowling—pages 27, 197, 232

Caroline Finnegan—page 104

Mathew B. Brady, Library of Congress Prints and Photographs—page 112 (*Susan B. Anthony*)

Brady-Handy Collection, Library of Congress, Prints and Photographs Division—page 78

Detroit Publishing Company Collection, Library of Congress Prints and Photographs—page 153

Dick DeMarsico, Library of Congress, Prints and Photographs Division—page 79 (*Martin Luther King Jr.*)

Gerhard Sisters, Library of Congress, Prints and Photographs Division—page 79 (*Jane Addams*)

William Hoogland, Library of Congress Prints and Photographs—page 111 (*Sequoyah*)

J.E. Purdy, Library of Congress Prints and Photographs—page 112 (*Clara Barton*)

Gilbert Stuart, Library of Congress Prints and Photographs—page 111 (*George Washington*)

Library of Congress Prints and Photographs—pages 111 (*Thomas Jefferson*) and 112 (*Thomas Edison, Wilbur and Orville Wright*)

Karl Schumacher, Library of Congress Prints and Photographs—page 113 (*Jimmy Carter*)

Courtesy of the family of Charles McGee—page 113 (*Charles McGee*)

Roger Morgan—pages 21 (*top*), 40, 43, 45, 46, 59–61 (*all*), 84, 189, 218 (*both*), and 242–246 (*all*)

NASA.gov—page 113 (*Neil Armstrong*)

Olivia Ogren-Hrejsa—pages 15, 50, 62, 102, 133, 136, 166, 169, 186, 191–192, and 226

Brian Payne—pages 58, 88, and 174

National Park Service, Independence National Historic Park, Charles Willson Peale—page 111 (*William Clark and Meriwether Lewis*)

R.A. Whiteside, Smithsonian Institute—page 163

Randy Piland—pages 52, 103 (*top*) and 164

Michael Roytek—pages 1 (*both*), 4–5, 6, 7 (*all*), 15, 19, 20, 22 (*both*), 53–54 (all), 64, 67, 68, 69, 70, 71–72 (*both*), 74, 76, 91 (*Cub Scout Six Essentials*), 134, 149 (*top*), 150, 152, 155-156 (*building dream catcher series*), 158 (*building talking stick series*), 160, 180, 188, 190, 195, 198, 201–203 (*all*), 219, 220–221, 224–225,

250, 253, 256, 257 (all), 262, 263–266 (all), 274, 275, 277–279 (all), 280, 283–284 (building mbira series), 286, and 288–290 (building rain stick series)

Notes

Notes

THE OUTDOOR CODE

As an American, I will do my best to—

- Be clean in my outdoor manners,
- Be careful with fire,
- Be considerate in the outdoors, and
- Be conservation minded.

LEAVE NO TRACE* PRINCIPLES FOR KIDS

Know Before You Go
Choose the Right Path
Trash Your Trash
Leave What You Find
Be Careful With Fire
Respect Wildlife
Be Kind to Other Visitors

*The member-driven Leave No Trace Center for Outdoor Ethics teaches people how to enjoy the outdoors responsibly. This copyrighted information has been reprinted with permission from the Leave No Trace Center for Outdoor Ethics: www.LNT.org.